Summer School '92

PROTECTING OUR PLANET

Activities to Motivate Young Students to a Better Understanding of Our Environmental Problems

For Primary Grades

by
Ava Deutsch Drutman

illustrated by Georgiann Gruenthaler

Cover by Jeff Van Kanegan

Copyright © Good Apple, 1991

ISBN No. 0-86653-619-1

Printing No. 987654321

Good Apple
1204 Buchanan St., Box 299
Carthage, IL 62321-0299

S I M O N & S C H U S T E R *A Paramount Communications Company*

P9-APO-490

DEDICATION

To my parents, Evelyn and Manne Deutsch, who have always supported me with love.

To my parents, Margaret and George Gruenthaler, with gratitude.

GA1338

TABLE OF CONTENTS

GA1338

INTRODUCTION

Children often overhear adults talking about environmental problems. Sometimes they are unable to understand the new environmental vocabulary. Often they are frightened by what they hear. Other times they want to help solve the problems, but do not know what to do. *Protecting Our Planet* was created to help children deal with the environmental problems we all face. This is done by providing facts about the problems and offering simple ways for children to contribute to the solutions.

Protecting Our Planet is divided into four chapters. "Our World" acquaints children with general information about the planet. This chapter is followed by "Air," "Water" and "Land." For simplicity's sake, the environmental problems have been placed in these chapters. It should be pointed out that some forms of pollution originate in one area and then float to another. For example, pollution can start on the land and float into the air and then eventually end in the water. Children need to realize that everything is connected. At times the reader will be referred to other pages in the book because of an extremely strong connection.

Protecting Our Planet is filled with a variety of word games and activities requiring a range of skills. Younger children may need assistance comprehending some environmental concepts. Some pages will introduce children to new concepts. Others will provide a vehicle for children to participate in solving environmental problems. It should be noted that due to the age of the children, most experiments will require adult assistance or close supervision.

On many pages, a new word about our environment is introduced. All these words appear in the glossary. Familiarity with scientific words is necessary for understanding many environmental concepts. A comfortableness with them in the primary grades will allow a fuller understanding of them as children mature. Encourage children to use the new word often so that it becomes part of their daily vocabulary.

At the end of the "Air," "Water" and "Land" chapters there are Protectors of the Planet awards. While each unit is studied, these awards should be given. Students should think of actions that classmates have taken to protect the air, water and land. They should then be given time to complete the awards appropriately. Encourage children to note friends' actions that positively affect the environment. The awards will encourage children to act in an environmentally concerned manner. If possible, children's names should be announced over the school public address system. This will encourage every child in the school to act in a similar manner toward the environment.

An answer key is provided only for those activities that have specific answers. Open-ended activities requiring children to use their creative thinking skills will produce a variety of responses. Children should be encouraged to share their ideas. If possible, allow children to put their ideas into action. Currently, national attention is focused on environmental issues. As new events occur, discuss these new findings with them.

As a culminating activity, there is an environmental game called Protect Our Planet. This game includes a gameboard, Earth Cards, Environmental Trivia Cards and Number Cards. The Environmental Trivia Cards require children to recall information about the environmental issues presented.

Sometimes the idea of environmental problems can be disturbing to children. Stress that things can be changed. It is our hope that *Protecting Our Planet* will arm children with the information necessary to truly make a difference.

GA1338

OUR WORLD

1

GA1338

YOUR ENVIRONMENT

NEW WORD: ENVIRONMENT

You have heard the word *environment* often. What does it mean? It means everything that surrounds you, the things you can see, touch, smell, hear or taste. But there are also some things that you cannot sense. Your environment is everything living. It is also the things that are not living. You have an environment in your home and outside of your home. Your environment affects the way you live. What is in your environment?

Think carefully about your indoor environment. Now list the things in your environment in each column. Now do the same for your outdoor environment.

INDOOR ENVIRONMENT

Things I Can See	Things I Can Hear	Things I Can Taste
_____	_____	_____
_____	_____	_____
_____	_____	_____

Things I Can Smell	Things I Can Feel	Things I Can Sense
_____	_____	_____
_____	_____	_____
_____	_____	_____

OUTDOOR ENVIRONMENT

Things I Can See	Things I Can Hear	Things I Can Taste
_____	_____	_____
_____	_____	_____
_____	_____	_____

Things I Can Smell	Things I Can Feel	Things I Can Sense
_____	_____	_____
_____	_____	_____
_____	_____	_____

GA1338

Now draw a picture of your indoor and outdoor environments. Include the things that you put on your lists. Make sure to include things that are living. Don't forget the things that are not living.

INDOOR ENVIRONMENT

OUTDOOR ENVIRONMENT

CAN YOU FEEL IT?

NEW WORD: ATMOSPHERE

We don't think a lot about the air. We feel it when the wind blows. Some days we see clouds in it. Other days we see rain or snow. Scientists use a special word for air. The word is *atmosphere*. The atmosphere is made up of different gases. It also has water vapor, dirt, pollen and dust in it. The atmosphere surrounds our planet. It protects the earth. The atmosphere has many layers. Space rockets travel through the atmosphere to reach other planets.

All our weather happens in the layer closest to earth. Look at the picture of our atmosphere below. Each circle shows a different layer of our atmosphere. Each layer has a name. Find the name and read a fact about it. Now find the layer closest to the earth. Draw pictures that show different kinds of weather.

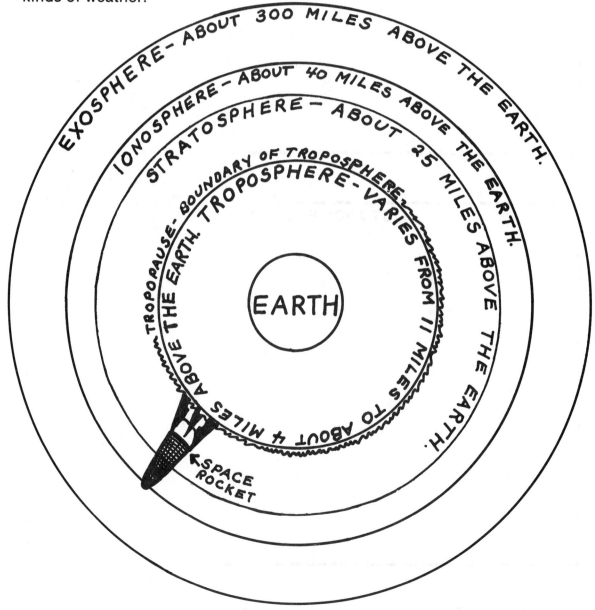

POLLUTION POINTS

NEW WORD: POLLUTION

Everyone does not live in the same environment. Some environments have more *pollution* than others. Pollution is when there are harmful things in the environment. These things can damage the planet.

We can find pollution in our water. We can find it in our air. It is also on the land. Pollution is in the city. It is in the country. Pollution can be found in many different places.

Here are the names of nine different places you might find pollution. Write each word on one line of the puzzle. Write only one letter in each box.

air
fields
rain

ponds
oceans

streams
roads

mountains
valleys

Discuss with your friends other places you might find pollution.

GA1338

EPA HIDE AND SEEK

NEW WORD: ENVIRONMENTAL PROTECTION AGENCY (EPA)

Our government wants to protect the environment. There is a special group that works to do this. The name of it is the *Environmental Protection Agency*. It is also called *EPA*. The *E* is for *Environment*. The *P* is for *Protection*. The *A* is for *Agency*.

The Environmental Protection Agency has a very important job. It helps plan our government's views toward the environment. It studies the environmental problems we have. It also works to control them. The EPA also provides information about many environmental problems—those in the air, in the water and on the land.

Can you find the Environmental Protection Agency hidden below? Sometimes it is written as the EPA. It is watching our air, water and land.

6

GA1338

AIR

7

IS AIR POLLUTION A PROBLEM?

Do you think we have pollution in our air? The answer is yes. The pollution causes problems for people. Five different problems are written in code below.

A	B	C	D	E	F	G	H	I	J	K	L	M	N	O	P	Q	R	S	T	U	V	W	X	Y	Z
1	2	3	4	5	6	7	8	9	10	11	12	13	14	15	16	17	18	19	20	21	22	23	24	25	26

1. Air pollution can cause __ __ __ __ __ __ __ __ __
    9 20 3 8 25   5 25 5 19

2. Air pollution can make it __ __ __ __ __ __ __ __ __ __ __ __ __.
    8 1 18 4   20 15   2 18 5 1 20 8 5

3. Air pollution can __ __ __ __ __ __ __ __ __.
    8 1 18 13   3 18 15 16 19

4. Air pollution can cause __ __ __ __ __ __ __ __.
    4 9 19 5 1 19 5 19

5. Air pollution can __ __ __ __ __ __ __ __ __ __ __
    8 1 18 13   15 21 20 4 15 15 18

    __ __ __ __ __ __ __ __ __ __ __ __ __ __
    15 2 10 5 3 20 19   20 8 1 20   13 1 14

    __ __ __ __ __.
    2 21 9 12 20

Now you know some of the problems caused by air pollution. People, animals and plants can be harmed by it. For years people have been aware of air pollution. Many things have been done to help end air pollution. Still more work is needed to end this problem.

8

SEEING IS BELIEVING

Do you think your air is free of pollution? Let's check it.

WHAT YOU WILL NEED

a piece of solid plastic (Plexiglas)
clear vegetable oil

WHAT YOU SHOULD DO

1. Coat the plastic with the oil.
2. Place outside a window.
3. Do not move the plastic for one day.

WHAT DID YOU LEARN?

_____

_____

_____

WHY DO YOU THINK THIS HAPPENED?

_____

_____

_____

WHY DID THIS HAPPEN?

You already know that some gases pollute the air. Some kinds of air pollution are tiny pieces of things. They can be dust, pollen, soil or even chemicals. They can be anything that floats in the air. Usually we cannot see them. Now we can see them trapped on the plastic.

Do you have a microscope nearby? Ask an adult to help you use it. It will show you the tiniest pieces in the air.

WHAT ELSE CAN YOU DO?

Prepare the plastic in the same way. This time place the plastic in different places. Could you put it near a busy corner? Could you put it in a park? Does the plastic look any different? Keep checking.

GA1338

FROM THE LAND INTO THE AIR

NEW WORD: FOSSIL FUELS

We all breath the air. Sometimes the air is not clean. It can have dirt in it. Air can have fumes mixed in it. Wind and rain help clean the air. People must help keep the air clean, too.

Sometimes there is a lot of air pollution. Where does it come from? Some air pollution is formed when *fossil fuels* are burned. Fossil fuels are fuels which usually are found underground. They are usually formed from dead plants and animals. Some fossil fuels are coal, oil and natural gas.

Sometimes we see air pollution. It looks like smoke. Other times we smell it. Sometimes we cannot sense it is there at all.

Most air pollution is formed on the land. The gases formed mix with the air we breathe. We burn fossil fuels when we ride in our *cars. Motorcycles* and *trucks* burn fossil fuels as they move. Some *trains* use fossil fuels, too. Many *factories* and *power plants* burn them. Some *businesses* and *homes* burn them to create heat. Fossil fuels are burnt in many places. Can you think of any other places?

Look at the word search. Find the sources of air pollution caused by burning fossil fuels. All the sources are italicized in the preceding paragraph.

```
T A O O Z Z N P Z M
R C P T F G B O I O
U I F H A H P W G T
C N A F R M S E W O
K V C A R S N R M R
S Q T A E M O P L C
B H O M E S N L M Y
D E R E L U A A R C
J K I T R A I N S L
R D E C O M S T W E
B U S I N E S S E S
```

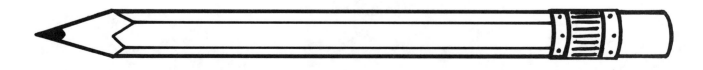

GA1338

THE HOLE IN THE SKY

NEW WORD: OZONE LAYER
NEW WORD: ULTRAVIOLET RAYS

Scientists found a hole in the *ozone layer*. The ozone layer is high above us. It is in our atmosphere. We cannot see it, but it has a very important job. It keeps out most of the harmful rays of the sun. These rays are called *ultraviolet rays*. Too many of these rays can cause people to become ill. They can cause sickness in some animals, too. The ultraviolet rays can cause certain plants to die also.

You might wonder where the hole is in the ozone layer. There is one hole over the North Pole. There is another one over the South Pole. The holes have been seen in the spring and fall.

Look at the picture below.

Find the sun. Color it yellow.

Find the ultraviolet rays. Color them purple.

Find the ozone layer. Color it blue.

Find the earth. Color it green. (Do not color the North or South Pole yet.)

Find the North Pole. Color it red.

Find the South Pole. Color it orange.

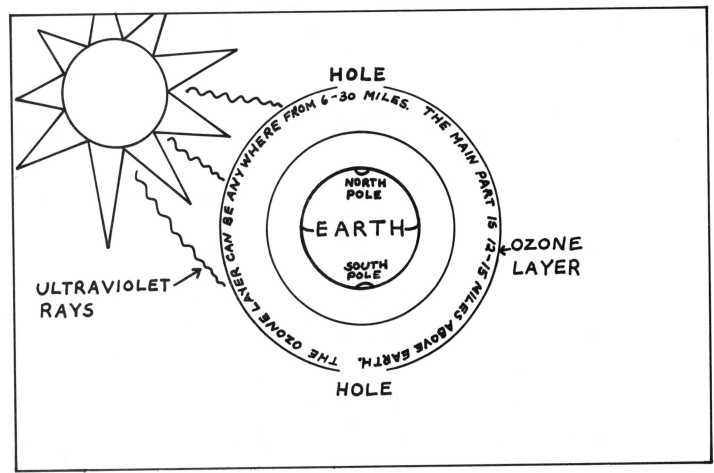

GA1338

CRAZY CFC'S

NEW WORD: CHLOROFLUOROCARBONS OR CFC'S

Chlorofluorocarbons are chemicals created by man. They are also called *CFC's*. When man invented CFC's, he was very pleased. CFC's could be used in air conditioners. They could be used in refrigerators. They could be used to make foamed plastics. They could be used for special spray cans. The CFC's remained unchanged when close to the earth.

Then the chlorofluorocarbons floated up and up. Something strange happened higher in the atmosphere. Scientists discovered that CFC's were harming our environment. They were creating the hole in the ozone layer.

Look for items that have CFC's labels on them. The label might say chlorofluorocarbons, also. Remember to read the labels. Circle all the things that have chlorofluorocarbons in them.

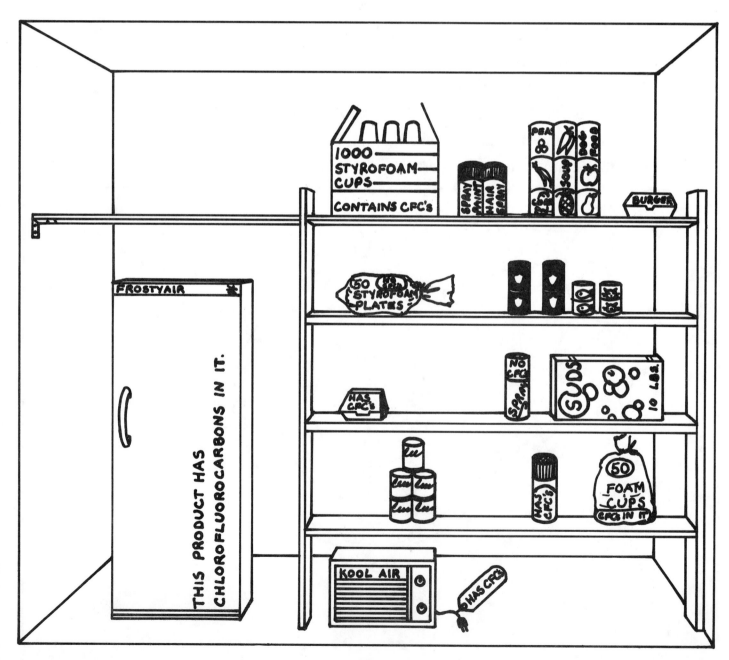

12

GA1338

CRY OUT AGAINST CHLOROFLUOROCARBONS

Since 1970 people have cried out against chlorofluorocarbons. People do not want a hole in the ozone layer. They have learned they must stop using chlorofluorocarbons. Not using CFC's means the ozone layer can be saved.

In 1987 twenty-seven countries signed a special treaty. They planned to lower the amount of CFC's. That treaty was called the Montreal Protocol. Today fewer and fewer CFC's are made. Our government is working hard to end the use of CFC's.

Some companies are finding ways to replace CFC's. They are making new chemicals to use instead.

People are still fighting against CFC's. Each sentence below has one vowel missing. Add the vowel to each word. Then you will know what they are doing.

Missing Vowel	
i	1. People stopped buy ___ ng a ___ r cond ___ t ___ oners for the ___ r homes.
a	2. They buy c ___ rs without ___ ir conditioners.
u	3. People check labels to see if prod ___ cts have CFC's. They do not b ___ y prod ___ cts that have them.
e	4. P ___ opl ___ r ___ cycl ___ CFC's from a r ___-frig ___ rator or air condition ___ r.
o	5. Pe ___ ple have t ___ ld their g ___ vernments that they are against CFC's.

You know many ways to help. Choose one of the ways. Use the space below to tell about it. Show it to other people. Explain what you have learned.

CROSSING CFC'S

Read each clue. Then write the answers in the right spaces. *Remember only one letter in each box*. Use the words below.

air conditoner   ozone   chlorofluorocarbons

refrigerator   spray   plastics   ultraviolet

ACROSS

1. Too many _____ rays come to earth through the hole.

3. *CFC's* means _____.

5. The _____ that keeps your food cold has CFC's in it.

DOWN

2. The _____ that cools your home has CFC's in it.

4. CFC's have caused a hole in the _____ layer.

6. Certain kinds of _____ cans have CFC's in them.

7. Foamed _____ have CFC's in them.

14

A WARMER EARTH?

NEW WORD: GLOBAL WARMING

Some people are worried about *global warming*. This means the temperature of the planet is getting warmer. Why does this matter?

Earth does not change its temperature very much. A warmer planet could mean many changes. These changes could take place very quickly. People, animals and plants might be harmed.

Read each sentence about global warming. One word is scrambled in each. Unscramble the word to find out what could happen. Write it on the line next to the scrambled word.

1. A warmer planet might cause all the ice to melt. Melting ice might create too much water. This might cause LFODOING _____.

2. Global warming might cause extreme changes in our EAEHRTW _____.

3. There may be too little rain. Then there might not be enough AERTW _____.

4. Certain plants and animals might move to new places. They are not able to ILVE _____ where they are now.

5. Some farmland might not be useable. People may have to MRAF _____ on different parts of the planet.

These changes may not occur. Scientists are still studying global warming. What else might happen if the planet became very hot? Write your ideas on the lines below.

_____
_____
_____
_____
_____
_____
_____

We must all understand how we add to global warming. If we understand it, then we can stop it.

HOT, HOT, HOT!

NEW WORD: GREENHOUSE EFFECT
NEW WORD: GREENHOUSE GASES

People are causing earth's atmosphere to warm. We do this in many ways. One way is by burning fossil fuels. The burning forms gases. We cannot see these gases. We *can* feel their effect. These gases cause the temperature of the planet to rise. Too many of these gases cause the *greenhouse effect*. Many people call this global warming.

What is the greenhouse effect? Did you ever leave your car in the hot sun? How does it feel when you get in it? It is hot. The sun's energy was trapped in the car. You feel that energy as heat. That is the greenhouse effect. It is when the sun's energy is trapped.

The greenhouse effect works the same way on earth.

Can you finish each sentence below? Use the words in the box.

escape	rise	heat
greenhouse gases		greenhouse effect

HOW THE GREENHOUSE EFFECT HAPPENS

The sun warms our planet. We feel the sun's energy as _____.

Now our atmosphere is filling with certain gases. These gases change our atmosphere. They trap the sun's energy. They are called _____.

Sometimes too much energy is trapped in our atmosphere. Then the temperature begins to _____ too high. The heat cannot _____.

We call this the _____.

Look at the picture below. It shows how the greenhouse effect happens on earth.

Find the sun. Color it yellow.

Find the earth. Color it green.

Find our atmosphere. Color it light gray.

Find the rays of the sun entering the earth's atmosphere. Color them orange.

Find the heat trapped in the earth's atmosphere. Color it red.

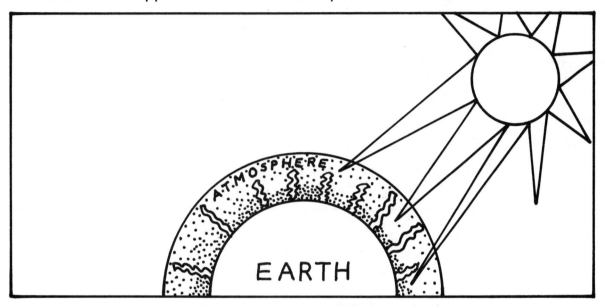

Now you know how the greenhouse effect happens. Use the space below to write it in your own words.

_____

_____

_____

_____

_____

_____

_____

_____

_____

_____

_____

_____

The cutting down of rain forests also adds to the greenhouse effect. Please see pages 106 and 107 to learn more about this.

                     GA1338

IT'S A GAS!

NEW WORD: CARBON DIOXIDE
NEW WORD: METHANE

You know that burning fossil fuels gives off a gas. We know it causes the greenhouse effect. But what is that gas called? It is *carbon dioxide*. A little carbon dioxide is always found in the air. Now man is making too much carbon dioxide. This amount traps the sun's energy. Carbon dioxide is a very important cause of the greenhouse effect.

Methane is another gas. It also traps the sun's energy. This helps cause the greenhouse effect, too.

The chlorofluorocarbons (CFC's) cause the greenhouse effect, also. The CFC's trap the sun's energy. Do you remember the CFC's? You learned that they hurt the ozone layer. CFC's are very dangerous to our atmosphere.

Let's learn a way that each gas is made.

Unscramble the words below. Now you know ways these gases are made. Which gas does each make? Find out by following the right path.

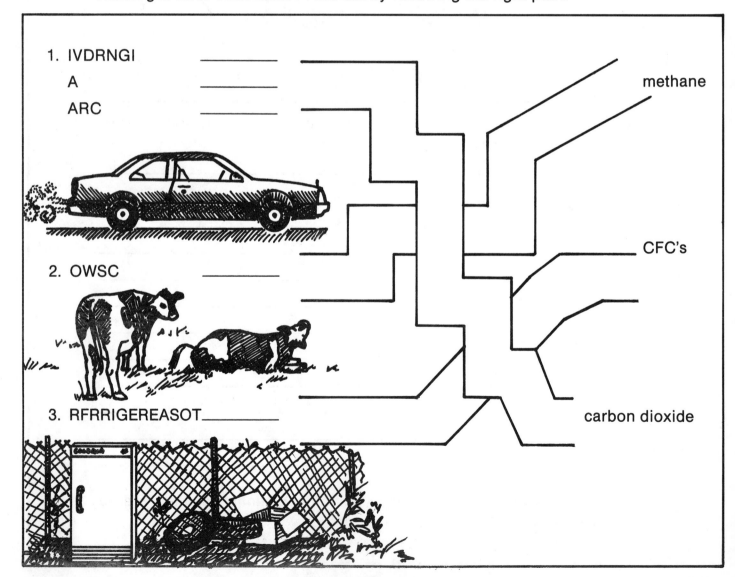

1. IVDRNGI _____
   A _____
   ARC _____

2. OWSC _____

3. RFRRIGEREASOT_____

methane

CFC's

carbon dioxide

18

GA1338

TRAPPING CHLOROFLUOROCARBONS

Refrigerators and air conditioners have chlorofluorocarbons in them. Sometimes CFC's leak out. Sometimes they escape during repairs. CFC's enter the air when a refrigerator is thrown away. It can happen to an air conditioner, too. All CFC's should be recycled.

Can you take *all* the chlorofluorocarbons to be recycled? Sure you can. Just follow the paths to do it. One path is for the CFC's from the air conditioner. Another one is for the refrigerator's CFC's.

GA1338

KEEP IT GREEN

What can cool the planet? Complete the dot to dot. Then you will know.

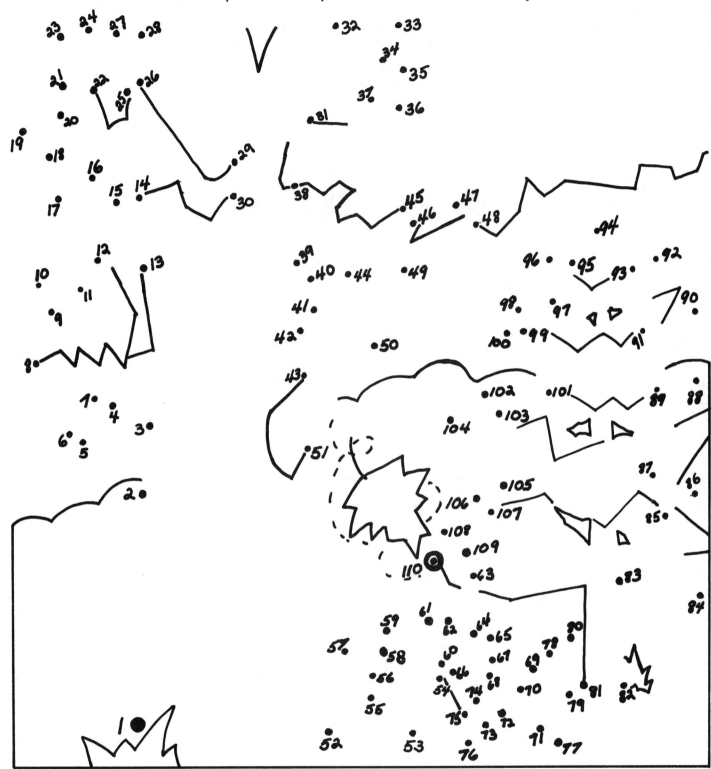

How do trees cool the planet? Too much carbon dioxide traps the sun's heat. This causes the temperature to rise. Trees use carbon dioxide to make food. This removes the carbon dioxide from the air. Trees also shade the planet. More trees mean a cooler planet.

20

A COOL IDEA

Trees help end global warming. They shade our earth. They remove carbon dioxide from the air. You can help by planting a tree. Ask an adult for permission before you begin.

WHAT YOU WILL NEED

a young tree   land for planting
a shovel   water

WHAT YOU SHOULD DO

GET READY

1. Dig a hole. It must be larger than the roots of the tree.
2. Soak the roots in water.
3. Loosen the soil at the bottom of the hole.
4. Spread out the roots.

PLANTING

1. Put the roots in the hole.
2. Put some soil around the roots.
3. Press the soil down.
4. Add more soil. Stop to press it each time soil is added.
5. Cover the roots totally.
6. Stop adding when you reach the tree's trunk.

WATERING

1. Water soil around the tree.
2. Keep the soil moist at all times.

GA1338

CRACK THE GREENHOUSE!

Global warming can be stopped. Our actions made the greenhouse effect. We can change. We can help our environment. Some children are already fighting against the greenhouse effect. They are using fewer fossil fuels. They are using less energy.

Use the code below. Then you'll know what they have done.

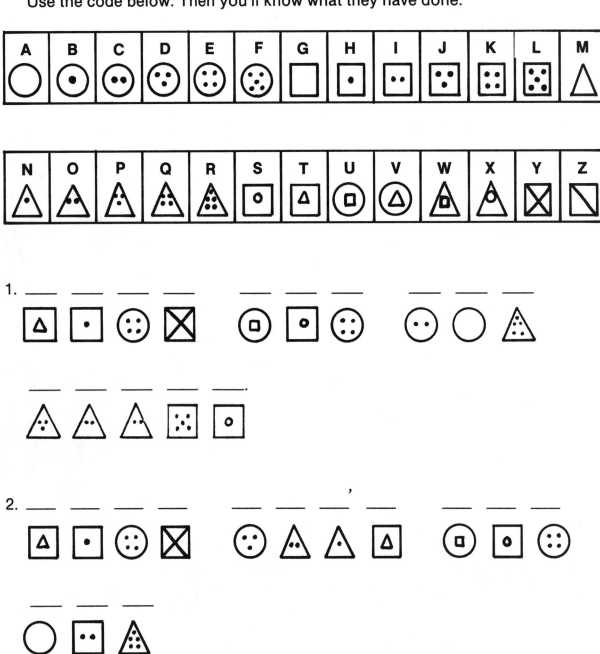

3. — — — — —   — — — — —   — — — — —

— — — — —   — — —   — — — — — —

4. — — — — —   — — — — —   — — — — —

— — —   — — — — — — — — — — — — —

— — — — .

5. — — — — —   — — — — — —   — — — — — —.

Can you think of other ways to help? Write them below. Discuss them with your friends.

_____

_____

_____

_____

_____

_____

_____

GA1338

WATCH OUT FOR THE ACID!

NEW WORD: ACID RAIN

It can harm plants and trees. It can harm animals. It can destroy the life in a lake, pond or stream. It can even cause damage to buildings. It doesn't sound like it is real, but it is. It is called *acid rain*.

Acid rain is a form of air pollution. It is created when fossil fuels are burned. Certain waste gases are formed during the burning. These gases mix with the water in the air. This makes acid rain. Acid snow is formed when the weather is cold. Acid rain is moved from place to place by the wind.

Acid rain falls on the land. It also falls in the water.

Look at the two pictures below. Find the changes caused by acid rain. Write the five changes on the lines below.

1. _____

2. _____

3. _____

4. _____

5. _____

GA1338

ACTION AGAINST ACID RAIN

Acid rain can be stopped in many ways.

1. Limit the amount of waste gases formed when burning fossil fuels.

2. Use scrubbers. These are special devices. They are put in smoke-stacks. When coal is burned, the waste gases go through smokestacks. The scrubbers remove harmful waste products. This helps prevent acid rain from forming.

3. Add limestone to places that have been hurt by acid rain. The limestone soaks up the acid. Soon the land and water will return to normal.

You know a great deal about acid rain. You can help these actions to be taken. Write to your local congressman or the President of the United States. Let him/her know your feelings about acid rain. You can make a difference!

Complete the letter below. If you choose, write your own letter. But don't forget to write!

_____
(date)

Dear _____,

   My name is _____. I live in_____

_____. I have heard

about the problem of acid rain. I know that acid rain _____

_____

_____.

   I would like to know how I can help. I would also like

you to _____

_____

_____

_____

_____.

   Thank you for taking the time to read my letter.

                    Yours truly,

_____
(your name)

GA1338

TRAFFIC EVERYWHERE

NEW WORD: SMOG

Lots of traffic and lots of sunlight give you *smog*. Most forms of transportation make gases when they move. Certain gases change when the sun shines on them. This forms smog. Smog is a form of air pollution. It happens when smoke and fog mix together. It is most often formed in cities that have lots of traffic. It happens when there is a great deal of sunshine. Smog is not good for people. It hurts the eyes and lungs. It is harmful to crops.

SMOKE + F**OG** = SMOG

Look at the picture below. Do you think there will be smog in this city today?_____ Circle all the things that contribute to smog in the picture.

GA1338

INDOOR AIR INSPECTORS

Are you an indoor air inspector? You can be one if you want! First you must know some *possible* causes of indoor air pollution. Go from circle to circle in straight lines to find some causes. Collect all the letters. Write them in their boxes. Then you will know some places indoor air pollution can start.

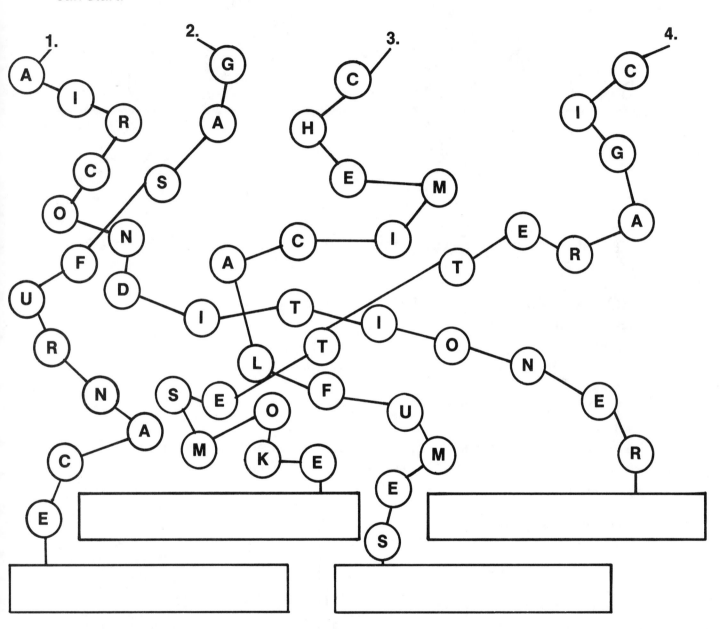

Now you know some places that indoor air pollution can start. The solution is written backwards. Turn it around and you will know one way to end indoor air pollution.

SROODNI   RIA   HSERF   HGUONE   PEEK

— — — — — — — — — — — — — — — — — — — —

27

PLANTS FOR CLEAN AIR

NEW WORD: POLLUTANT

Some plants can help end air pollution. Recently scientists have discovered this fact. These plants remove certain pollutants from the air. A pollutant is something that causes pollution. Here are two plants that help.

ENGLISH IVY   POTHOS

Plant at least one of these plants. You have helped clean the air. Here is how to do it.

HOW TO MAKE A CUTTING

WHAT YOU WILL NEED

a cutting   (Cut a piece from a plant that is already growing.
              Make sure it has a stem with leaves on it.)

a glass jar or bottle

soil (Potting soil is the best.)

water

a small plastic container (An empty yogurt container would be fine.)

a saucer (An empty aluminum pie tray would be excellent.)

a nail and hammer

HOW YOU WILL DO IT

Step 1

1. Remove the bottom leaves from the cutting.
2. Fill the glass jar with water.
3. Put the cutting in the jar.
4. Place near a sunny window.
5. Check daily to make sure the stem is covered with water.
6. Watch the roots grow.
7. Remove from the jar when the roots are 3" (7.62 cm) long. This should take about two weeks.

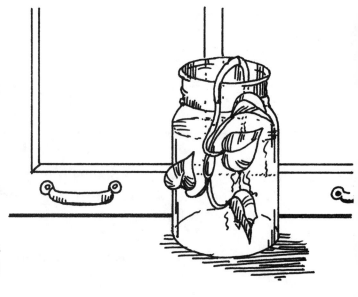

Step 2
(You can begin Step 2 while you watch the roots grow!)

1. Make a few holes in the bottom of the plastic container. Use the hammer and nail to do this. Ask an adult for help.
2. Put soil in the container. Fill almost to the top.
3. Move the soil around with your fingers.
4. Make a hole in the soil.
5. Place the cutting in it.
6. Pat the soil around it.
7. Water your plant. Check often to see if your plant needs water.
8. Transplant your plant when it outgrows the container.

HINTS FOR HEALTHY PLANTS
English ivy needs lots of sun. Keep the soil moist.
Pothos does not need lots of sun. Let the soil dry before you water it again.

You've just helped clean the air. You helped the environment in another way. Just think of how many things you reused. You saved them from becoming garbage. Can you list them below?

_____

_____

_____

_____

Now you know plants can end air pollution. Where are some places you might want to put these plants? List the places below.

_____

_____

_____

_____

GA1338

DANGER ZONE

Sometimes air pollution comes from chemicals. They get into the air in different ways. Look at the mixed up pictures below. Cut out each box. Put them together to make a clear picture. Then paste them in the correct boxes on page 31. Now you know three ways that chemicals get into the air.

1. Airplane spraying crops to get rid of bugs or weeds.
2. Fumes leaking from a container that has a poison symbol on it.
3. Fumes coming from a factory-like building.

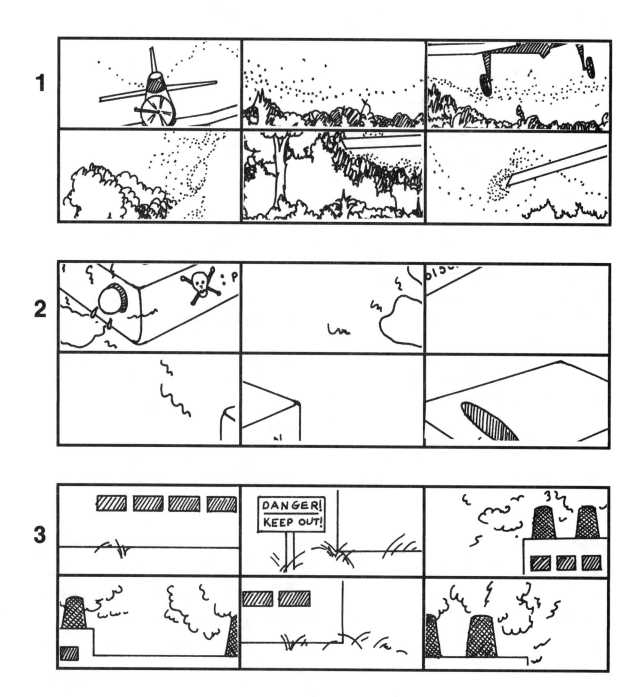

GA1338

Sometimes factories give off chemical fumes.

Some chemicals come from protecting our crops.

Some products have chemical fumes.

No one wants chemicals in the air. These chemicals can be dangerous. Everyone wants clean air. Laws help end air pollution. The Environmental Protection Agency works for clean air. There are no easy answers. We have to work together. We *can* end air pollution!

31

GA1338

YOU'RE TOO NOISY

One kind of air pollution is clean. It does not have a chemical in it. There are no harmful fumes. It will not add to the greenhouse effect. It won't hurt the ozone layer. What is it? It is *noise pollution*. Too many very loud sounds can harm people. It can hurt your hearing. Don't worry. It only happens if you listen for too long of a time.

Here are some kinds of noise pollution. Start at each number. Follow the straight lines from square to square. Collect all letters to find them. List the kinds of noise pollution below.

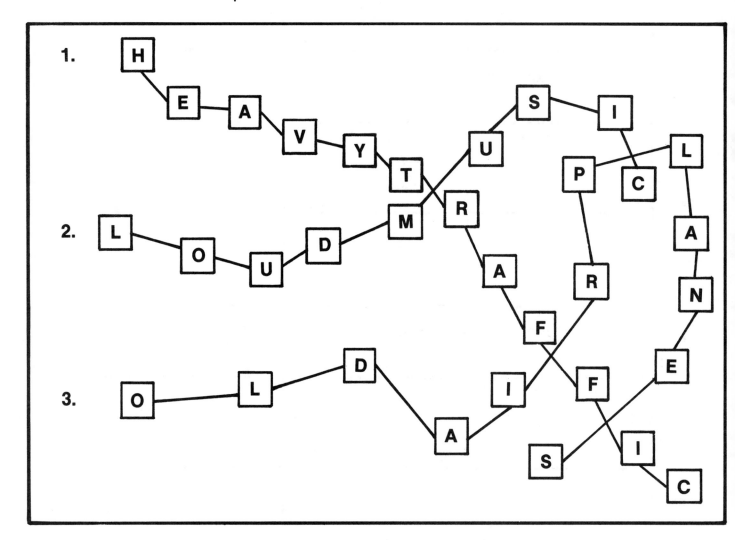

Can you think of at least two more? Add them to the list.

1. _____

2. _____

3. _____

4. _____

5. _____

GA1338

HIDING IN THE AIR

Not all air pollution is the same. There are different causes of air pollution. Can you find these hiding in the air below?

chemical fumes   acid rain   smog
carbon dioxide   CFC's   noise
methane

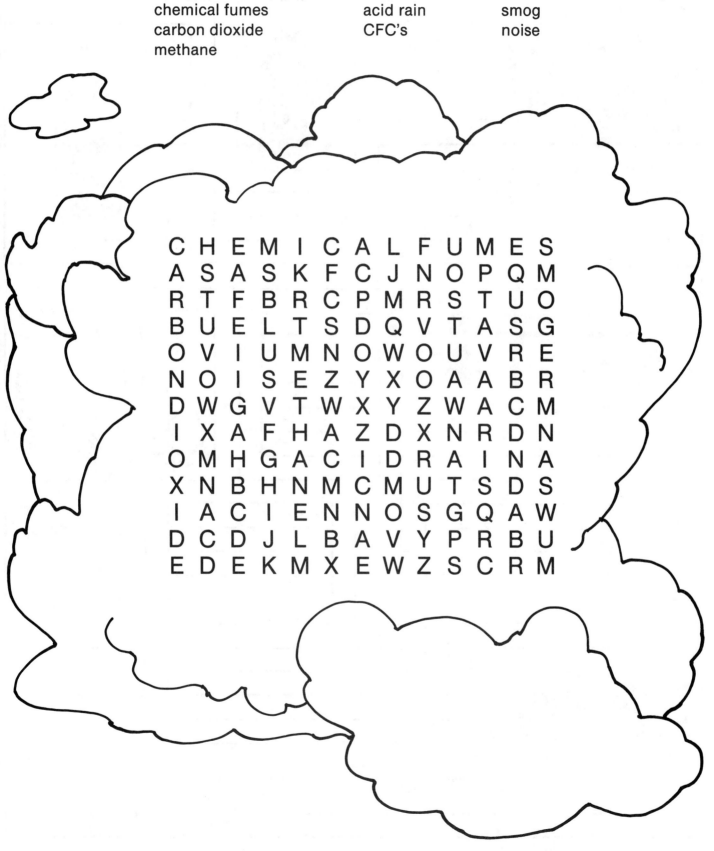

```
C H E M I C A L F U M E S
A S A S K F C J N O P Q M
R T F B R C P M R S T U O
B U E L T S D Q V T A S G
O V I U M N O W O U V R E
N O I S E Z Y X O A A B R
D W G V T W X Y Z W A C M
I X A F H A Z D X N R D N
O M H G A C I D R A I N A
X N B H N M C M U T S D S
I A C I E N N O S G Q A W
D C D J L B A V Y P R B U
E D E K M X E W Z S C R M
```

33

GA1338

FREE AIR

Watch out for the air pollution. Can you help clean air find its way to your house? Follow the path that has NO pollution on it.

34

GA1338

CLEAN AIR VS. DIRTY AIR

NEW WORD: CLEAN AIR BILL

Our government wants to help end air pollution. This is done by passing laws. The laws have been called the *Clean Air Bills*. The first Clean Air Bill was passed in 1963. The Clean Air Bill tells people everything they must do to end air pollution. Several Clean Air Bills have been passed since 1963. The most recent one was passed in 1990.

People have thought of different ways to keep the air clean. Here are some of them.

- Cars create a lot of air pollution when they burn gasoline. The Clean Air Bills required makers of cars to end that. They had to create a way for the engines to pollute less. They did.

- Burning coal creates air pollution. Many homes, industries and means of transportation used to burn coal. The burning of coal has been lessened by Clean Air Bills.

- Some industries create air pollution as they make things. The Clean Air Bills have asked certain industries to stop polluting. They have ended some problems. They are working on the more difficult ones.

Imagine that you could write your own Clean Air Bill. Complete these sentences with your ideas about air pollution. Try to think of real causes of air pollution. How would you solve the problem? Would you write to the President of the United States? Would you start an organization to end air pollution? Would you write ideas in a newspaper? How would you get your Clean Air Bill passed?

I want the air clean because _____

_____

_____

_____

To end air pollution, I think we should _____

_____

_____

_____

_____

I would include all this in my Clean Air Bill. I would pass my Clean

Air Bill in _____.

GA1338

CLEAN AIR ACTIONS

People all over the world are working to end air pollution. Now cars pollute less than in the past. Many factories prevent harmful gases from reaching the air. Our government has passed many laws to end air pollution. We must all work together. You can help end air pollution, too.

Look at the picture by each sentence. Each sentence tells about actions you can take. The vowels are missing in each sentence. Add the vowels to discover how you can help. Try to do each action.

a	e	i	o	u
●	*	∞	□	■

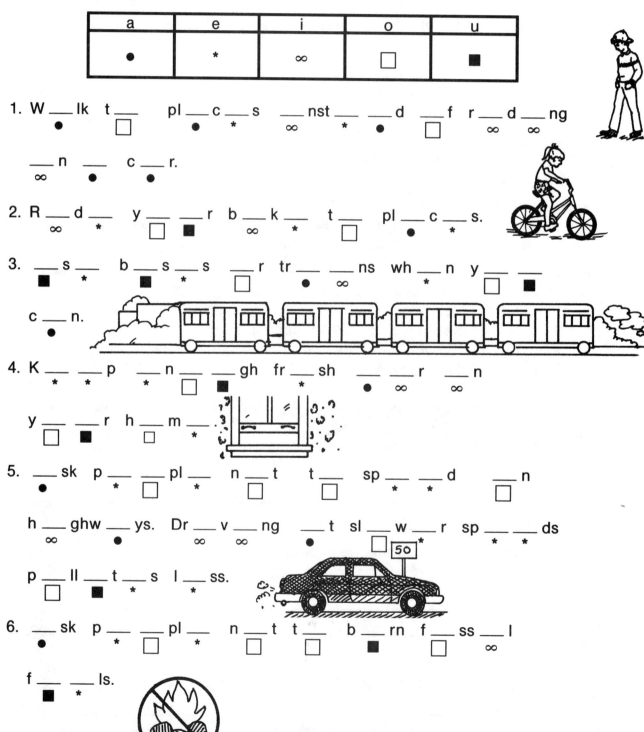

1. W __ lk t __ pl __ c __ s __ nst __ __ d __ f r __ d __ ng
   ● □ ● * ∞ * ● □ ∞ ∞

   __ n __ c __ r.
   ∞ ● ●

2. R __ d __ y __ __ r b __ k __ t __ pl __ c __ s.
   ∞ * □ ■ ∞ * □ ● *

3. __ s __ b __ s __ s __ r tr __ __ ns wh __ n y __ __
   ■ * ■ * □ ● ∞ * □ ■

   c __ n.
   ●

4. K __ __ p __ n __ __ gh fr __ sh __ __ r __ n
   * * * □ ■ __ * ● ∞ ∞

   y __ __ r h __ m __
   □ ■ □ *

5. __ sk p __ __ pl __ n __ t t __ sp __ __ d __ n
   ● * □ * □ □ * * □

   h __ ghw __ ys. Dr __ v __ ng __ t sl __ w __ r sp __ __ ds
   ∞ ● ∞ ∞ ● □ * * *

   p __ ll __ t __ s l __ ss.
   □ ■ * *

6. __ sk p __ __ pl __ n __ t t __ b __ rn f __ ss __ l
   ● * □ * □ □ ■ □ ∞

   f __ __ ls.
   ■ *

GA1338

Which action do you think is most important? Make a poster about it. Display the poster. Let others know how they can help end air pollution.

GA1338

NOT THE USUAL

Everyone wants to end air pollution. Some people have found ways to help. They do not burn fossil fuels to make electricity. They do not pollute to make heat. They use other ways to make energy, ways that do not pollute our earth—ways that are found in nature. We must use them carefully. Then they can last forever.

Look at the pictures. Unscramble the words. Then draw a line from the word to its picture.

1. aflilgn   atrew

   _____   _____

2. uns

   _____

3. inwd

   _____

4. enaco   eenryg

   _____   _____

5. eath rfom iisden het aerht

   _____ _____ _____ _____ _____

Imagine you are building a factory. You do not want to pollute. What kind of energy will you see? _____

Why did you choose this kind? _____

_____

_____

38

GA1338

AIRING IDEAS

Help everyone learn facts about air pollution. Make your own air pollution bulletin board.

What should you put on your board? Here are some ideas.

FIGHTING AIR POLLUTION

Look in newspapers and magazines for stories about air pollution. Cut out the most interesting ones. Paste them on the board.

Ask friends to write their ideas about ending air pollution. Place their ideas on the board.

Have a poster contest. Call it Clean Air Fighters. Put the best drawings on the board.

TREES ARE OUR FRIENDS.

Have different parts of the board for the different air pollution problems. Use titles like these:

- Acid Rain
- Global Warming
- The Hole in the Ozone Layer
- Smog

Have friends write facts about each one.

Invite people to make a machine that would clean the air. Tell everyone to use his/her imagination. Hang the best machine on the board.

GA1338

CARE ABOUT AIR

Create your own mobile. It will tell everyone about cleaning the air. A cool breeze moves your mobile. Read one of the idea shapes. Remember to do it. Maybe the next breeze will have no pollution in it.

WHAT YOU WILL NEED

poster board
yarn
scissors
glue
crayons or markers
hole punch

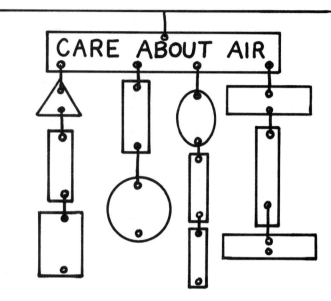

WHAT YOU SHOULD DO
CUTTING AND PASTING
1. Cut out the Care About Air strip.
2. Paste it on the poster board.
3. Read all the ideas in the shapes.
4. Cut out the ideas you like the best. (You can make your own idea shapes, too.)
5. Paste your idea shapes on the poster board.
6. Cut out all the shapes and strips.
7. Cut one piece of yarn 12" (30.48 cm) long.
8. Cut eight pieces of yarn 8" (20.32 cm) long.

COLORING
1. Color all the idea shapes.
2. Draw a picture that shows the idea on the back of each shape.

PUNCHING HOLES
1. Punch a hole at the top of the Care About Air strip. Punch four holes at the bottom.
2. Punch holes at the top and bottom of each idea shape.

PUTTING IT ALL TOGETHER
1. Use the 12" (30.48 cm) piece of string. Put it through the top hole of the Care About Air strip.
2. Use the 8" (20.32 cm) pieces to attach the idea shapes to the mobile.
3. Hang your Care About Air mobile where everyone can see it.

GA1338

CARE ABOUT AIR

Tell others about getting energy from the sun.

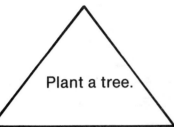

Plant a tree.

Write to someone about ways to end air pollution.

Ride a bike instead of driving a car.

Take a train or bus instead of driving a car.

Don't use any products with CFC's in them.

Don't leave the refrigerator open.

Save energy.

Try not to use toxic products.

Write to the EPA. Find out ways you can help end air pollution.

Tell people that CFC's can be recycled.

YOU'RE ON THE AIR!

You and a friend are going to be on the radio! You will ask questions about air pollution. Your friend will answer them. If possible, tape the interview. Play it for your school.

Here are some questions. Add other questions. Use all the facts you know about air pollution!

FIGHT AIR POLLUTION TODAY!

Question: Why are you interested in fighting air pollution?

Answer: _____

Question: Why do you believe air pollution is a problem?

Answer: _____

Question: What can we do to end air pollution?

Answer: _____

Question: Why is the greenhouse effect happening?

Answer: _____

Question: Can we end the greenhouse effect? How?

Answer: _____

Question: Will you explain how smog is made? Why is it a problem?

Answer: _____

Question: What is acid rain?

Answer: _____

Question: _____

Answer: _____

Question: _____

Answer: _____

Question: _____

Answer: _____

Question: _____

Answer: _____

42

GA1338

AIR AIDES

Do you want to know more about air pollution? Do you want to know other ways to end air pollution? Here are the names of two groups that help to end air pollution. Write to one of the groups. Ask for more information about the problem. Find out more about fighting air pollution.

National Clean Air Coalition
801 Pennsylvania Avenue S.E., 3rd Floor
Washington, D.C. 20003

How does air pollution change our environment? This group can help you find the answer. They will help you find a local group. Maybe they could help you start your own.

Office of Air and Radiation
United States Environmental Protection Agency
Washington, D.C. 20460

This is a government agency. It looks at the quality of air in our country. It has many booklets about air pollution. They can answer all your questions.

Below is the beginning of a letter. Add your ideas. Then mail it.

_____, 19 ___

_____

_____

Washington, D.C. _____

Dear _____,

  I want air pollution to be stopped. I am writing to you because

_____

_____

_____

_____

_____

_____

_____

Thank you very much.

Yours truly,

_____

GA1338

PROTECTORS OF THE PLANET

Now you know ways you can protect the air. Complete the awards below. Then cut them out. Color them too. Give them to people who deserve them.

Complete the list on page 45 by writing the name of the person and the reason for the award. If possible, hang up the list and encourage others to read it.

Look everywhere for people who are protecting our air.

Name

Reason for Award

GA1338

IMAGINE

Imagine you live in a world without any air pollution. What would it be like? Write or draw about your world. You learned how air pollution is caused. You know the causes of

- global warming
- the hole in the ozone layer
- smog
- acid rain
- indoor air pollution
- noise pollution

Think carefully before you begin! Remember that you do not want to cause air pollution. How would you travel? How would you heat your home? Which things wouldn't be made any more? Would your world be very different? Imagine . . .

GA1338

WATER

47

GA1338

WATER WORRIES

Water pollution causes problems. Connect the dots. Then you will know who and what can be harmed.

Water pollution can destroy

1. _____

It can destroy other sea animals, too.

Water pollution can harm

2. _____

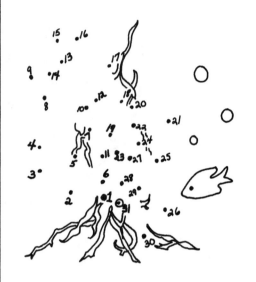

3. Water pollution can cause _____ to feel ill. It can also cause them to have deadly diseases.

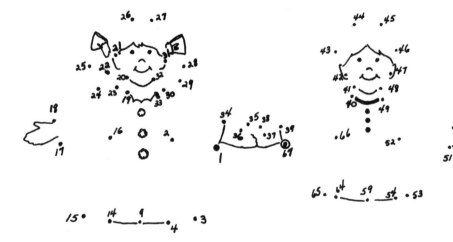

GA1338

WATER, WATER EVERYWHERE

NEW WORD: FRESH WATER
NEW WORD: SALT WATER

Taste the water in the ocean. Just a little drop! "Wow! That sure is salty!" you say. The water in the oceans and seas is *salt water*. This water has large amounts of salt in it. Would the water in a pond taste salty? Probably not. Pond water is usually *fresh water*. Fresh water does not have salt in it. Certain sea creatures and plants can live only in salt water. Fresh water is needed by others. Fresh water and salt water meet at some places. Pollution can be found in salt water or fresh water. A large part of our earth is covered with water. Two thirds of the water is salt water.

Water can be found in many different places. Can you find all the places hidden in the puzzle?

swamp	ocean	bay	brook	pond
stream	marsh	sea	river	lake

```
S  T  R  E  A  M  M  M
E  A  I  E  F  J  A  A
A  B  V  G  M  L  R  R
C  H  E  N  T  A  S  S
D  B  R  O  O  K  H  H
I  A  P  O  C  E  K  K
X  Y  Q  W  E  L  S  S
Z  R  E  R  A  V  T  T
A  M  P  O  N  D  U  U
S  W  A  M  P  L  R  R
```

Can you think of any others? List them below.

_____

_____

_____

GA1338

AROUND AND AROUND

NEW WORD: WATER CYCLE
NEW WORD: EVAPORATION

Water goes around and around. It falls to the earth. It becomes part of our land and water. Then it rises back into the air. This is called the *water cycle*. It is the endless path water takes. How does water rise back into the air? The water must turn into a gas. *Evaporation* is the way water turns into a gas. You can make this happen yourself.

WHAT YOU WILL NEED

a small bowl that you can see through
   (plastic or glass)
water to fill the bottom of the bowl
clear plastic wrap

WHAT YOU SHOULD DO

1. Fill the bottom of the bowl with water.
2. Put the plastic wrap over the top of the bowl.
3. Place the bowl in direct sunlight.

WHAT DID YOU LEARN?

_____
_____
_____

WHY DO YOU THINK THIS HAPPENED?

_____
_____
_____

WHY DID THIS HAPPEN?

The sun's heat caused the evaporation of the water in the bowl. It rises up onto the plastic *sky*. Then it turns to *rain*. The *rain* falls back into the *pond* below. This happens during the water cycle.

GA1338

Look at the picture below. Follow the directions.

Find the clouds. Draw rain, snow, sleet or hail falling from the clouds. Find the land. Draw lakes, streams, rivers, swamps, marshes or ponds on it.

THE WATER CYCLE

evaporation from

ponds, lakes, streams, swamps, marshes, rivers, streams, oceans, trees, plants

Now you have a drawing of the water cycle.
Trace the movement of the water from earth back up to the sky. Then trace it back down to earth again. You will see it go around and around.

TROUBLED WATER

NEW WORD: SEWAGE
NEW WORD: SLUDGE
NEW WORD: FERTILIZER
NEW WORD: PESTICIDE

Why does that water smell so horrible? Why is it so dirty? Here are some common causes of water pollution. Read each clue. Then unscramble the words. Now you know some of the causes!

1. This is very often dumped in the ocean. It is made of thrown-away things. It is AGAEGBR.

   _____

2. It is a waste. Water carries it into the sewers. It is called SEEAGW. (Hint: It is a NEW WORD.)

   _____

3. People use it on their gardens. It is also used on farms. It protects crops from bugs. It is picked up by rainwater. It is called a SPTIEICED. (Hint: It is a NEW WORD.)

   _____

4. This is the garbage from some industries. It comes from some factories. It can look like dirty water. It is very dangerous. It is HCEIMALC SATEW.

   _____

5. It is left after sewage is treated. It looks like mud. It is called SDLGEU. (Hint: It is a NEW WORD.)

   _____

6. It is used to heat our homes. It is used to run our cars. It is carried in tankers. It is ILO.

   _____

7. It is used to make many things. A milk container is made from it. A drum to hold chemicals is made from it. These are made of LAPSTCI.

   _____

8. Some people use this on their lawns. It is also used on farms. It helps crops and lawns grow. It is picked up by rainwater. It is called RFEEZRIITL. (Hint: It is a NEW WORD.)

   _____

GA1338

UNDER THE GROUND

NEW WORD: GROUNDWATER

After it rains, where does all the water go? Some of it goes into lakes, streams, rivers or oceans. Some of it goes into the soil. The water goes underground. It becomes *groundwater*.

Imagine you are a raindrop. You don't want to get polluted. Only one path doesn't have pollution on it. Keep the groundwater clean.

53

GA1338

RED ALERT!

NEW WORD: HAZARDOUS WASTE

Stay away from that garbage! It is *hazardous waste*! It may look like dirty water. But it is much more dangerous. It is harmful to people, plants and animals. It can poison you. It can burn you. It can explode. It can destroy things.

Are you wondering how it gets into the water? Sometimes hazardous waste is dumped into our water. It can be dumped in a river or lake. It can also be dumped into the ocean. Sometimes hazardous waste gets into the water through accidents.

Look at the picture below. Can you find the hazardous waste getting into the water? Circle each one. Then list them below.

1. _____
2. _____
3. _____
4. _____

Hazardous waste is very dangerous. What do you think it does to the sea creatures? What do you think it does to plants? Write your ideas below.

_____
_____
_____
_____

GA1338

Can you prevent hazardous waste from getting into our water? You can help. You can write to the people who make the laws. You can tell them how you feel about it. Write your letter below.

Here are some ideas for your letter.
- Write about what you know.
- Write your ideas about keeping hazardous waste out of our water.
- Ask for more information about hazardous waste in the water.

You can use these ideas. You can add others. You can choose to write a different letter. Just let your ideas be known!

—————————, 19 ——

——————————

——————————

Dear ————————————,

   I have learned that hazardous waste is dangerous. I know that it can ——————————————————————————
——————————————————————————
——————————————————————————
——————————————————————————
——————————————————————————

   I do not want hazardous waste in the water. I think ——————
——————————————————————————
——————————————————————————
——————————————————————————

   I want to know more about hazardous waste. I would like to know
——————————————————————————

Thank you for reading my letter.

Yours truly,

——————————————————————————

GA1338

A DANGEROUS SEARCH

NEW WORD: HAZARDOUS WASTE DISPOSAL CENTER

Read the list below. All these things can be dangerous. You may have some in your home. Look for them with an adult. Read the label on each. Check to see if the EPA says they are hazardous. Can you find them hidden in the puzzle?

bleach   cleaners   paints   gasoline

motor oil   pesticides   mothballs

```
A C L E A N E R S D E
B A U V B C D E F M P
L G A S O L I N E A A
E S M W M N G H O P I
A M O T O R O I L Q N
C T S A I J K R S T T
H P E S T I C I D E S
R M O T H B A L L S M
```

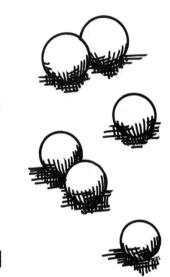

Adults must be careful when using hazardous products. People must be careful with the waste, too. As garbage it becomes hazardous waste. We must keep it out of the water. We shouldn't throw it into a sink. We should never rinse it away with water.

The waste should be taken to a *hazardous waste disposal center*. This is a place where hazardous waste is taken. Here it is taken care of in the right way. It does not get into our water. The EPA can tell you about a hazardous waste disposal center near you.

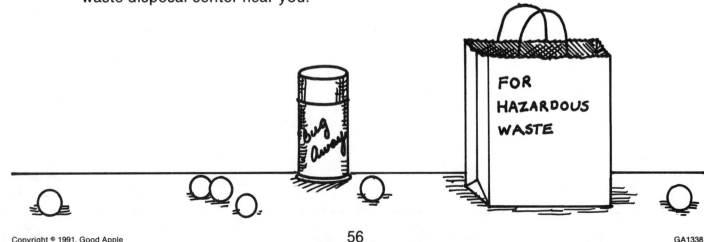

GA1338

IT'S TIME FOR A CHANGE

What if you didn't want to use hazardous products? What would you use? Here are some ideas. None of these are hazardous.

baking soda   vinegar   borax   lemons

Here are ways to use them. Count the number of letters in each word. Match the number of letters to the number of boxes. Then you will know what to use.

1. Does someone want to clean a window? Is the glass cleaner hazardous? Use this instead.

    2 tablespoons (30 ml) of ☐ ☐ ☐ ☐ ☐ ☐ ☐ in 1 quart (.96 l) of water

    +

    or

    2 tablespoons (30 ml) of ☐ ☐ ☐ ☐ ☐ in 3 cups (720 ml) of water

    +

2. Does someone need to remove grease? Is he going to use a hazardous product? Tell him that he can use these instead.

    ☐ ☐ ☐ ☐ ☐ ☐

3. Does someone need to clean an oven? Ask him to use this instead of a hazardous product.

    ☐ ☐ ☐ ☐ ☐ ☐   ☐ ☐ ☐ ☐ and water

    +

4. Does someone need to clean the bathroom? Ask him to use this. It will not harm the environment.

    ☐ ☐ ☐ ☐ ☐ ☐   ☐ ☐ ☐ ☐ on a damp sponge. Scrub. Then rinse with water. Finally shine with a clean cloth.

    +   +   +

5. Is the drain in the sink clogged? Someone can fix it with these.

    ¼ cup (60 ml) of ☐ ☐ ☐ ☐ ☐ ☐   ☐ ☐ ☐ ☐ and ½ cup (120 ml) of ☐ ☐ ☐ ☐ ☐ ☐ ☐

    +

RUNAWAY

NEW WORD: RUNOFF

Rain brings water to earth. Sometimes we use water to clean things. We water our crops. We use water in industry. Sometimes water travels along the land. The water is called *runoff*. When it moves, it picks up things along the way. Sometimes it gets polluted. Follow the right path. Help the rainwater stay clean.

GA1338

WATCH OUT BELOW!

NEW WORD: GUTTER
NEW WORD: STORM DRAIN

You see these all the time. They have water in them. Did you know this water can be dangerous?

Start at the first letter in a circle. Then go from circle to circle. Follow the straight lines. Write all the letters in the box. Then you will know what they are.

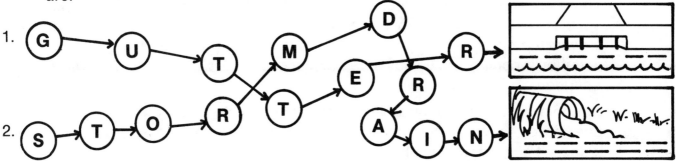

You wonder how the water can be dangerous? Use the pictures to help you understand.

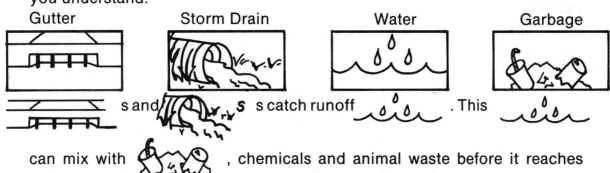

Gutter   Storm Drain   Water   Garbage

s and   s catch runoff   . This

can mix with   , chemicals and animal waste before it reaches

them. This is polluted

Sometimes there is   in these   s and   s.

When the   mixes with the   you have more pollution.

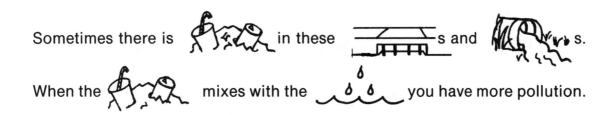

When   is polluted it can make you sick. Stay away from

s and   s. Remember to tell your friends about this.

GA1338

DID YOU KNOW THIS?

NEW WORD: NONPOINT SOURCE POLLUTION

It's raining. It's pouring. Oh no! I just changed the oil in my car. There is oil on the ground. The rain washes away the oil.

It's raining. It's pouring. Oh no! I just took my dog for a walk. I didn't clean up his waste. The rain washes it away.

These are two ways that water gets polluted. The runoff from the rain picks up the oil. It also picks up the dog waste. This runoff goes into a lake, a river, the ocean or the groundwater. It takes the pollution with it. Water pollution is coming from many different places. This is called *nonpoint source pollution*.

Nonpoint source pollution is a real problem. A little pollution comes from one place. A little comes from another place. It is hard to stop because it doesn't come from one place.

It is important to understand nonpoint source pollution. Everyone can make a difference.

Read the sentences in each box. Put an *X* on the causes of nonpoint source pollution.

Ken is washing his car. He uses very little soap on his car. He only turns on the hose when he needs it.

James is oiling his lawn mower. He leaves the oilcan open. It spills on the driveway. James uses his hose to wash it away.

Ken is cleaning his chair. He is using a hazardous product. He is careful not to spill it. He throws the waste away properly.

GA1338

James is painting his table. He is using a kind of paint that is hazardous. He doesn't use all the paint. He pours the waste into his pond.

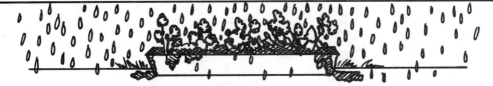

James hears it will rain. He pours on more fertilizer than usual. He doesn't want it to wash away in the rain.

Ken listens to the weather. He hears it will rain. He decides not to fertilize his garden. He knows the fertilizer will be washed away.

James is fishing today. He eats a snack on the boat. He throws his garbage into the water.

Ken is in his boat. He eats lunch on the boat. He keeps his garbage. He will throw it away properly.

Who is not causing *nonpoint source pollution*? _____

What can you do to end nonpoint source pollution? List your ideas below.

_____

_____

_____

_____

_____

GA1338

LAKE CARE

How do you know if a lake needs your help? Look at the picture below. This is a lake that needs *you*.

This lake is in trouble. Here are some clues that tell you this. Circle each clue as you find it.

- There are no fish living here.
- There are no frogs here.
- Runoff is coming into it.
- The water is not clear.
- The water has suds in it.
- There is garbage floating in it.
- It is filled with fallen branches and leaves.

This lake can be helped. Here's what can be done.

- Take care of the plants that grow there.
- Plant more trees and plants.
- Remove the garbage.
- Remove the branches and leaves.
- Keep people and animals away from the edge of the lake.
- Call the EPA to report the problem.

Can you think of other ways to help? Write them below.

_____

_____

_____

_____

Imagine that all the work on the lake is finished. Look at the pictures below. Create your own clean, clear lake. Cut out the pictures below. Paste them in or around the lake. Add your own creatures and plants.

63

GA1338

REALLY CARING

Some lakes are really in trouble. You know the clues of a troubled lake. You know how to help it too. Walk around your neighborhood with an adult. Look for a lake that is in trouble. *You can really care for it*!

First get permission from an adult. Ask others to help you. You will need one adult to work with you. Tell others what you know about lakes. Plan what you will do.

Put up a sign by the lake. It will explain what you are doing. It may get other people interested. Here are some ideas you might put on your sign.

- the name of the lake
- what needs to be done to clean it
- when you will be doing the work

You can make a difference. Good luck!

Plan your sign in the space below.

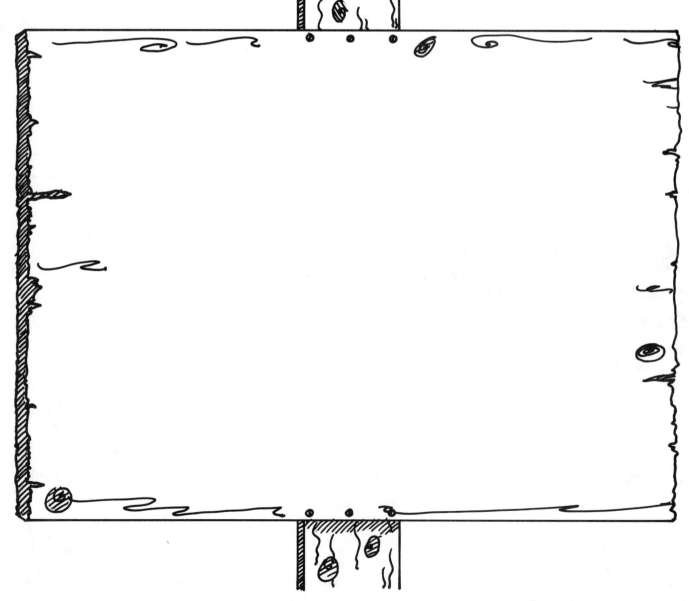

GA1338

WHAT A MESS!

Tankers carry millions of gallons (liters) of oil. These huge boats travel across the ocean. Sometimes an accident happens. This causes the oil to spill into the ocean. Sea creatures and plants are harmed. The coast can be damaged too.

An oil spill is difficult to clean up. Many ways have been tried. Use the code. Add the correct vowels to each word. Now you know some of the ways.

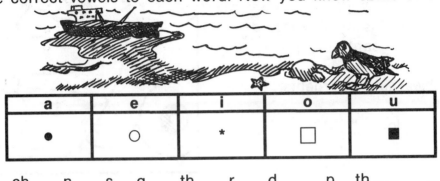

a	e	i	o	u
●	○	*	□	■

1. M __ ch __ n __ s g __ th __ r __ d __ p th __ __ __ l.

2. St __ n __ s __ l __ ng th __ sh __ r __ w __ r __ w __ p __ d by h __ nd.

3. Ch __ m __ c __ ls w __ r __ __ s __ d t __ br __ __ k __ p th __ __ __ l.

4. P __ __ pl __ w __ sh __ d th __ __ __ l __ ff s __ __ __ n __ m __ ls.

5. B __ rd __ rs w __ r __ pl __ c __ d __ r __ __ nd __ n __ __ l sp __ ll. Th __ s k __ pt __ t fr __ m spr __ __ d __ ng.

Each oil spill is different. The cleanup must be different too. Sometimes the cleanup uses many different ways. So far no one way works on all oil spills. Everyone hopes for one wonderful way to do it. They hope the way will work every time. They hope it will work quickly. Scientists are working on these new ways. Have you heard of any?

Can you think of ways that oil spills could be prevented? Write your ideas below.

_____

_____

_____

GA1338

AN OIL SPILL AT HOME

—Ask an adult to help with this experiment.—

WHAT YOU WILL NEED

one large bowl

one measuring cup

water

motor oil **Warning:** Motor oil is hazardous. Handle with care!

rubber gloves

different dishwashing detergents

paper towels

small pieces of cloth

sponges

string

WHAT YOU SHOULD DO

1. Fill half of the bowl with water.
2. Put on rubber gloves. (This will protect your hands from motor oil.)
3. Measure ¼ cup (60 ml) motor oil.
4. Carefully add the motor oil to the water.
5. Gently shake the bowl to create "waves."
   - Did the oil and water mix? _____
6. Try to clean up the oil with a paper towel.
   - Did it work? _____
7. Gently shake the bowl to create "waves."
8. Try to clean up the oil with a piece of cloth.
   - Did it work? _____
9. Gently shake the bowl to create "waves."
10. Try to clean up the oil with the string. Make a border around it.
    - What shape is the border? _____
    - Did the oil stay in the border? _____
11. Use the string to try different border shapes.
12. Gently shake the bowl to create "waves."
13. Try to clean up the oil with each detergent.
    - Did they work? _____
    - Which one worked the best? _____
14. Gently shake the bowl to create "waves."
15. Try to clean up the oil with the sponge.
    - Did it work? _____

WHAT DID YOU LEARN?

_____

_____

_____

_____

GA1338

WHY DO YOU THINK THIS HAPPENED?

_____

_____

_____

_____

WHY DID THIS HAPPEN?

Each oil spill is not the same. Different ways of cleanup are needed for each spill. What works for one may not work for another. Sometimes more than one way is needed to clean up an oil spill.

Try two different ways without shaking the bowl. Write what happened below.

The Two Ways Tried	What Happened?
_____	_____
_____	_____

Can you think of any other ways to clean up the oil? Can you blow the oil apart? Can you scoop it up? List your ideas below. Try each one. Write what happened.

A Way to Clean Up Oil	What Happened?
_____	_____
_____	_____
_____	_____

Drop a small plastic toy into the bowl. Drop a stone into it? Does the oil get on the toy? Does the oil get on the stone? How can you clean these? Write what happened when you tried.

A Way to Clean Up Things	What Happened?
_____	_____
_____	_____
_____	_____

What happens to real sea creatures during an oil spill? What do you think happens to the nearby land? How might we protect them? Write your ideas below.

_____

_____

_____

LET'S GO TO THE BEACH

NEW WORD: POLLUTANT

What a great day at the beach! We could all go in the water. Oops! No we can't. I see some *pollutants*. Each one of them pollutes the water in a different way. Can you find the pollutants at the beach? Circle each thing that does not belong at the beach.

Did you find seven pollutants? These are only a few pollutants you might see. Have you ever seen any others at the beach? Some water pollutants we cannot see. They disappear in the water. We must work together to end water pollution at our beaches.

Can you do anything to end beach pollution? Write your ideas below.

_____

_____

_____

SAVE A DROP

Do you ever waste water? Do you throw unused ice cubes into the sink? Then you have wasted water. You can use ice cubes to water plants. You can choose to save water each day. Read the list below. Keep track of the ways that you save water. Add a drop to your chart each time you save water.

Note: A gallon (3.78 l) of water would fill this milk jug.

Ways to Save Water	Water Saved	Number of Times You Saved Water
Shower for less than five minutes.	About 15 gallons (56.7 l) of water will be saved.	
Take a shower instead of a bath.	About 10 gallons (37.8 l) of water will be saved.	
Don't let any faucet leak.	About 30 gallons (113.4 l) of water will be saved in one day.	
Don't let the water run while you brush your teeth.	About 10 gallons (37.8 l) of water will be saved.	
Don't fill the sink with water when washing hands.	About 5 gallons (18.9 l) of water will be saved.	
Flush the toilet when necessary.	About 5 gallons (18.9 l) of water will be saved each time you don't flush the toilet.	

Can you think of other ways to save water? How many gallons (liters) of water do you think will be saved? Write your ideas below.

Ways to Save Water	Water Saved	Number of Times You Saved Water
_____	_____	_____
_____	_____	_____
_____	_____	_____
		_____

DRIP, DRIP, DRIP

Look at the house below. Water is being wasted. Can you find the waste? Circle each way it is being wasted. Then list the ways below. How could the water have been saved? Write your idea next to each one.

	Water Waste	**Ways to Save the Water**
1.	_____	_____
2.	_____	_____
3.	_____	_____
4.	_____	_____
5.	_____	_____
6.	_____	_____

WATER DETECTIVES

How do you use water? List four ways.

1. _____
2. _____
3. _____
4. _____

What holds water in your home? Where do you get water to drink? Look around your home. List three.

1. _____
2. _____
3. _____

Sometimes water leaks out of these things. Each leak wastes water. How much water is wasted? Only you can find out! Here's how to do it?

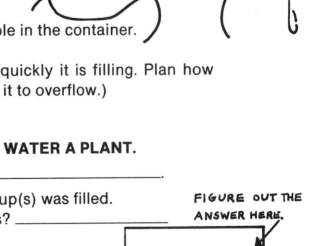

WHAT YOU WILL NEED

a real leak
a plastic container of water
a measuring cup (the one-cup [240 ml] size)

HOW YOU WILL DO IT

1. Find the leak, or using a nail, make a *tiny* hole in the container.
3. Put the measuring cup under the leak.
4. At first, watch the cup carefully. See how quickly it is filling. Plan how often it should be checked. (You don't want it to overflow.)
5. Write the information below.

USE THE WATER YOU GATHER TO WATER A PLANT.

The water is leaking from _____.

In one hour, _____ measuring cup(s) was filled.

How much water would be wasted in two hours? _____

FIGURE OUT THE ANSWER HERE.

Here is the way to know the answer.
Add the number that you wrote two times.

How much water would be wasted in one day? _____

FIGURE OUT THE ANSWER HERE.

Here is the way to know the answer.
There are twenty-four hours in a day.
Add the number that you wrote twenty-four times.

GA1338

CLEAN AND CLEAR

NEW WORD: WATER TREATMENT PLANTS
NEW WORD: FILTRATION
NEW WORD: AERATION
NEW WORD: CHLORINE

People have discovered how to clean "dirty" water. Now water can be reused. Cleaning it is very important. You might wonder why it is important?

- In some places people do not have enough water to drink. "Dirty" water is cleaned. This same water is then used as drinking water.
- In other places there isn't any clean water. "Dirty" water must be cleaned. It can then be used.
- Farmers always need water for their crops. Sometimes there isn't enough rain. "Dirty" water must be cleaned. Then it must be reused.

Can you think of other reasons that "dirty" water must be cleaned? Discuss them with your friends.

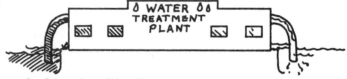

Read each sentence below. It will tell you ways to clean water. The name of each is in code. Can you figure out each name?

A	B	C	D	E	F	G	H	I	J	K	L	M	N	O	P	Q	R	S	T	U	V	W	X	Y	Z
1	2	3	4	5	6	7	8	9	10	11	12	13	14	15	16	17	18	19	20	21	22	23	24	25	26

1. Places have been set up to clean water. These places can remove chemical wastes. They can take animal waste out of the water. These places remove the germs that cause disease. They are called

   $\overline{23}\ \overline{1}\ \overline{20}\ \overline{5}\ \overline{18}$ $\overline{20}\ \overline{18}\ \overline{5}\ \overline{1}\ \overline{20}\ \overline{13}\ \overline{5}\ \overline{14}\ \overline{20}$ $\overline{16}\ \overline{12}\ \overline{1}\ \overline{14}\ \overline{20}\ \overline{19}$.

2. Sometimes water is poured through fine sand or charcoal. These remove the harmful substances in the water. This is called

   $\overline{6}\ \overline{9}\ \overline{12}\ \overline{20}\ \overline{18}\ \overline{1}\ \overline{20}\ \overline{9}\ \overline{15}\ \overline{14}$.

3. Sometimes air is put in water. This extra air cleans the water. This is called

   $\overline{1}\ \overline{5}\ \overline{18}\ \overline{1}\ \overline{20}\ \overline{9}\ \overline{15}\ \overline{14}$.

4. Adding certain chemicals cleans water. The most common one is called

   $\overline{3}\ \overline{8}\ \overline{12}\ \overline{15}\ \overline{18}\ \overline{9}\ \overline{14}\ \overline{5}$. It is used in swimming pools. It keeps the water fresh.

Now you know how much water would be wasted in a day. Can you find out how much water would be wasted in two days?

Remember: Tell an adult if this is a real leak. It needs to be fixed. *Water conservation* begins at home.

GA1338

CLEANUP ACTIONS

NEW WORD: CLEAN WATER ACT
NEW WORD: SAFE DRINKING WATER ACT

Our government wants clean water for everyone. In 1899 the first clean water law was passed. It was called the Refuse Act of 1899. It told people not to dump things into water. There have been other laws since then.

A strong law was passed in 1972. It was called the *Clean Water Act*. The goal of this law was to make all the lakes and rivers clean. It has caused the water to be cleaner. The Clean Water Act prevents things from being dumped in the water. The law gave money to help clean up the water. There are special laws just to protect the oceans.

In 1974 a law to protect drinking water was passed. It was called the *Safe Drinking Water Act*. In 1986 new ways to end water pollution were added. The law was passed again.

What has gotten into our water? List the three water pollutants.

1. _____

2. _____

3. _____

At times industry dumps its waste into the water. Cities have been known to throw their garbage into the water also. There has been poisonous runoff from farms.

The Environmental Protection Agency (EPA) helps to make sure people obey the laws. It also studies water pollution. The EPA protects our environment. It helps plan the laws. The EPA has a very important job.

Imagine you work for the EPA. How would you keep our water clean? How would you get people to obey the laws? What laws would you pass? Write your ideas below.

_____

_____

_____

_____

_____

_____

_____

_____

Discuss your ideas with your friends. Decide which ones you feel are the best. You might send those ideas to the Environmental Protection Agency.

GA1338

HELPFUL WAYS

Here are some ways to protect our water. They are written in code. Can you figure them out?

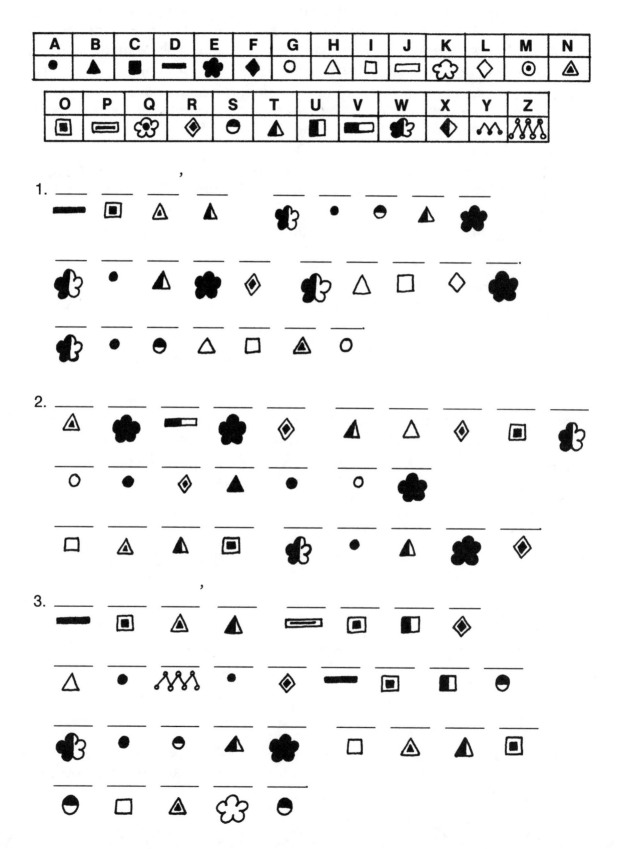

GA1338

4.
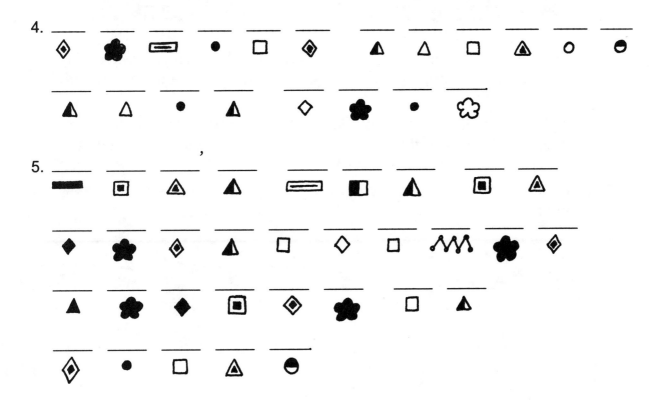

5.

Can you think of another one? Write it in code. Ask a friend to figure it out.

Your Idea in Code

A WATER CREATURE

You know Smokey Bear. He tells you to prevent forest fires. You know Woodsy Owl. He tells you not to pollute. These animals were made to remind you to protect our environment.

Who reminds us to keep our water clean? Who tells us to save water? Can you make a creature to do that? Should it be a fish? Should it be a dolphin? Should it be a drop of water? You decide!

Draw it below. Give it a name. What will it say? Hang your drawing where everyone can see it. Have friends create their own creatures.

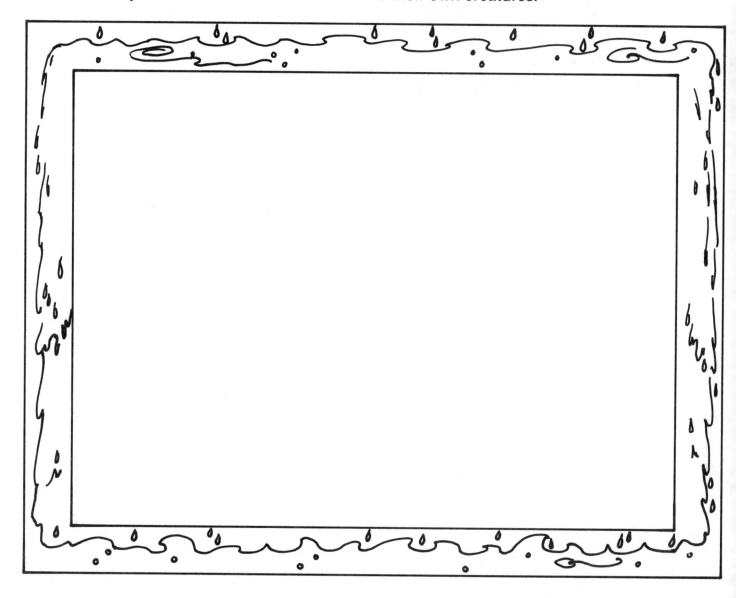

Here's an idea! Turn your creature into a puppet. Then put on a puppet show. It could be about keeping our water clean. It could tell others about ways to save water.

GA1338

PASS THE WORD

NEW WORD: WATER CONSERVATION

Is there enough clean water for everyone? Some people think there isn't. These people believe in *water conservation*. They do not waste water. They protect water. Water conservation is protecting and saving water.

Many people don't know how to save water. Some people don't know they are polluting water. You know the facts. Pass the word. Set up a water conservation stand in your school. First get permission from your school principal and teacher. Then begin working. Plan the way your stand will look.

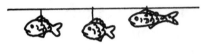

Make a list of ways to save water. Make a list of ways to prevent water pollution. Use all the facts you have learned. Show these facts to everyone.

Ways to Save Water

_____
_____
_____
_____
_____
_____

Ways to Prevent Water Pollution

_____
_____
_____
_____
_____
_____

To the President of the United States:

We want clean water. We think water conservation is very important. We feel there should be strong laws to protect our water.

_____ _____ _____
_____ _____ _____
_____ _____ _____
_____ _____ _____
_____ _____ _____

GA1338

WET WORDS

Make your own water book! What will you call it? What will you include in it?

Here are some ideas. Choose one or pick an idea of your own.

- Write about ways that water is used. Put one idea on each page. Draw a picture about it.
- Describe ways to save water. Write one way on each page.
- Make your own water puzzles and games.
- Describe ways to keep our water clean.
- Paste a news article about water on each page.

Cut out the pages below. Staple or sew the pages together. Put the title on the first page. Then add your ideas. Share the book with your friends.

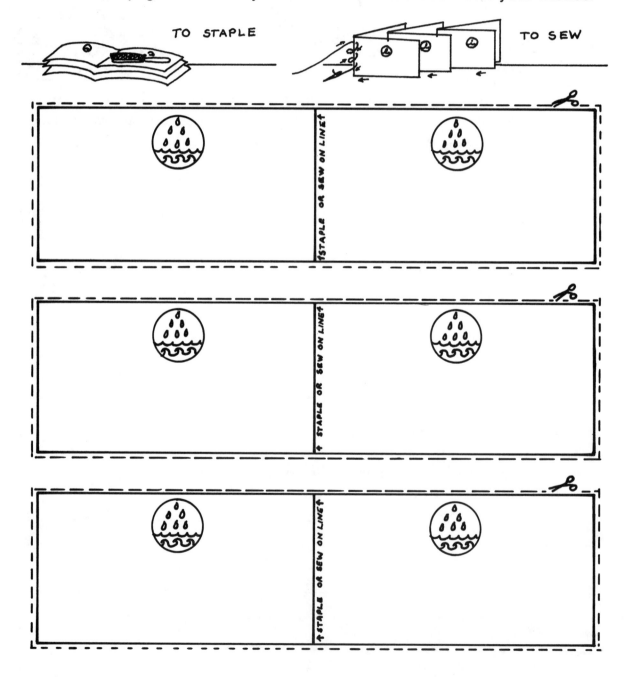

TO STAPLE

TO SEW

STAPLE OR SEW ON LINE

STAPLE OR SEW ON LINE

STAPLE OR SEW ON LINE

GA1338

WATER WATCHERS

Here are some groups that care about water. Some work to end water pollution. Others work for water conservation. Each group has its own goal. Which group interests you? Write to that group. They will tell you more about themselves.

The National Water Alliance
1225 1 Street N.W., Suite 300
Washington, D.C. 20005

This group teaches people about water. It also tries to get stronger laws to protect our water.

Clean Water Action
317 Pennsylvania Avenue, S.E.
Washington, D.C. 20003

This group works for clean, safe water.

Seacoast Anti-Pollution League
Five Market Street
Portsmouth, NH 03801

This group protects seacoast regions. It teaches people about threats to our shoreline.

How about starting your own group? What would you call it? What would your group do? Would you protect lakes and streams? Would you work to end water waste? Write your ideas on the lines below.

The name of my group would be _____

_____

We would meet on _____

_____

We would meet at _____

_____

Our group is interested in _____

_____

_____

We would do these things _____

_____

_____

GA1338

PROTECTORS OF THE PLANET

Now you know many ways to protect the water. Complete the following awards. Then cut them out. Color them too. Give them to people who earn them.

Complete the list on page 81 by writing the name of the person and the reason for the award. If possible, hang up the list and encourage others to read it.

This award is presented for protecting our water.

Name _____

Action taken _____

_____

_____

This award is presented for protecting our water.

Name _____

Action taken _____

_____

_____

This award is presented for protecting our water.

Name _____

Action taken _____

_____

_____

This award is presented for protecting our water.

Name _____

Action taken _____

_____

_____

Name   **Reason for Award**

GA1338

IMAGINE

Imagine you are a fish. Pretend that there isn't any water pollution. What would the world be like? Write a story about your pond. You can draw a picture about it instead. Remember that clean water wouldn't have any of these in it:

- sewage
- sludge
- fertilizers
- pesticides
- hazardous waste

Don't forget to think about these three words: *runoff, groundwater, nonpoint water pollution*

Think carefully before you begin! How different would the water cycle be? Would you notice anything different in runoff water? What would happen to drinking water? How would other sea creatures feel about the change? Would your world be very different? Imagine . . .

LAND

WE'VE LANDED

You're in the park. You're standing on land. You see plants growing out of the ground. Maybe you see animals who live there. You really don't think much about the land. You should! You can protect the land from harm. To do this you must know about the land.

Go outside or to a park. Look around your feet. Pick up a little soil.

Does it feel dry or wet? _____

How does it smell? _____

What color is it? _____

Does it have stones in it? _____

Is anything growing in it? _____

Are there any creatures in it? _____

REMEMBER: Please put the soil back where you found it. Pat it back gently into place.

Now look around you. Is the land flat or hilly? Do you see many trees growing on the land? Are there farms? Draw what you see.

GA1338

Have you ever traveled far from home? Does the land look the same wherever you go? What is the ground like at the beach? What is it like in a forest? Write the name of each place you have seen. Then write about how the land is different.

Place	**How the Land Is Different**
_____	_____
_____	_____
_____	_____
_____	_____

Land is not the same everywhere. But all soil is made of the same things. They are

- minerals like clay, sand or bits of rocks
- water
- air
- things that were once living

The amount of each thing makes the soil different. Soil has more minerals in it than anything else. Did you find any minerals in the soil you just held?

Look at the picture of the soil below. Can you find the different parts of the soil? Circle them in the picture.

GA1338

USE IT OR HARM IT?

What do we do on our land? Look at the pictures first. Then unscramble the words to find out.

1. We ULIBD _____ on it.

2. We raise OODF _____ on it.

3. We NEMI _____ it.

Do you do anything else on the land?

_____

_____

We can do all these things. But we must do them wisely. We must protect our land from harm. In the past we have not always been so careful.

How have we harmed our land? Look at the pictures first. Then unscramble the words to find out.

1. We destroyed LPANST _____ and EETSR _____ that protect our land.

2. We used OISL _____ in the wrong ways.

3. We INMED _____ the land carelessly.

4. We buried AZHRUSOAD _____ pollutants in the land.

5. We dumped GBAGREA _____ carelessly.

Have we harmed our land in other ways, too? _____

_____

LOOSE LAND

NEW WORD: EROSION

Erosion happens when soil is moved around. This causes the land to slowly wear away. Wind can blow the soil. Water can wash it away. Man can also cause it to happen. People must use land correctly. Then we can help prevent erosion.

Erosion can be a problem. It can hurt the land that is used to grow food. It can harm our water. It can damage our coastline.

WHAT YOU WILL NEED
sand (or completely dry soil)
a pan
water
water can

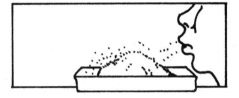

WHAT YOU SHOULD DO
1. Make a pile of sand in the pan.
2. Gently blow the sand. (People should not stand close to the sand.)

WHAT HAPPENED?

_____

_____

WHY DO YOU THINK THIS HAPPENED?

_____

_____

WHAT YOU SHOULD DO
1. Make a pile of sand in the pan.
2. Fill the watering can with water.
3. Sprinkle the top of the pile with water.

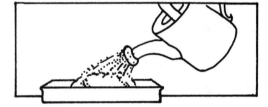

WHAT HAPPENED?

_____

_____

WHY DO YOU THINK THIS HAPPENED?

_____

_____

WHY DID THIS HAPPEN?
You caused erosion to happen. In the first part you created "wind." The "wind" moved the sand. This happened because the sand was not protected. In the second part you created "rain." The "rain" moved the sand. The sand was not protected.

HOW COULD YOU PROTECT THE SAND?
Would a wall stop the wind from causing erosion? Try putting a cardboard wall around it. What would stop the water from causing erosion? Think about ways to end erosion. Try them with your pile of sand. Do you think they would work in the real environment? Discuss your ideas with your friends.

GA1338

PERSONAL PAPERS

NEW WORD: LITTER

Sometimes people throw their garbage along the side of roads. That is called *litter*. Most people don't do that any more. Leaving garbage on a road pollutes the environment. It looks ugly. It might harm some animals. Some garbage pollutes the soil. Other garbage can pollute the water.

Every day you make garbage. For one day save the paper garbage you have made. Decide which garbage you could recycle.

GA1338

Look at the picture below and the one on the preceding page. They both look the same. Color one of the pictures to show a clean environment. Paste pieces of litter on the other picture. Now that environment is polluted compare the two pictures. How did the *litter* change the way the environment looks? Could the water be harmed by the *litter*? Could the animals be affected by the *litter*? What might it do to the soil? Are the plants and trees affected also? Discuss these ideas with your friends.

89

GA1338

THE LAND IS FULL

NEW WORD: LANDFILL

People used to put their garbage in town dumps. It smelled. It was ugly. It harmed the environment. The garbage caused air, water and land pollution.

Today we understand more about pollution. We no longer have dumps. Now we have *landfills*. Here our garbage is safely buried. Scientists study where it is safe to build a landfill. The land is protected from the garbage. Scientists are using their knowledge to protect our environment.

Now there is a new problem. We have more and more garbage. Many old landfills are *full*. There are only a few places to build new landfills.

What can we do? Some ideas are written in code. Can you find out what they are?

A	B	C	D	E	F	G	H	I	J	K	L	M
Z	Y	X	W	V	U	T	S	R	Q	P	O	N

N	O	P	Q	R	S	T	U	V	W	X	Y	Z
M	L	K	J	I	H	G	F	E	D	C	B	A

1. $\overline{\underset{F}{\quad}}\ \overline{\underset{H}{\quad}}\ \overline{\underset{V}{\quad}}\quad \overline{\underset{G}{\quad}}\ \overline{\underset{S}{\quad}}\ \overline{\underset{R}{\quad}}\ \overline{\underset{M}{\quad}}\ \overline{\underset{T}{\quad}}\ \overline{\underset{H}{\quad}}$

$\overline{\underset{Z}{\quad}}\ \overline{\underset{T}{\quad}}\ \overline{\underset{Z}{\quad}}\ \overline{\underset{R}{\quad}}\ \overline{\underset{M}{\quad}}\quad \overline{\underset{Z}{\quad}}\ \overline{\underset{M}{\quad}}\ \overline{\underset{W}{\quad}}$

$\overline{\underset{Z}{\quad}}\ \overline{\underset{T}{\quad}}\ \overline{\underset{Z}{\quad}}\ \overline{\underset{R}{\quad}}\ \overline{\underset{M}{\quad}}.$

2. $\overline{\underset{I}{\quad}}\ \overline{\underset{V}{\quad}}\ \overline{\underset{K}{\quad}}\ \overline{\underset{Z}{\quad}}\ \overline{\underset{R}{\quad}}\ \overline{\underset{I}{\quad}}\quad \overline{\underset{G}{\quad}}\ \overline{\underset{S}{\quad}}\ \overline{\underset{R}{\quad}}\ \overline{\underset{M}{\quad}}\ \overline{\underset{T}{\quad}}\ \overline{\underset{H}{\quad}}.$

GA1338

3. <u> </u> <u> </u> <u> </u>   <u> </u> <u> </u> <u> </u> <u> </u> <u> </u> <u> </u>
   Y   F   B   G   S   R   M   T   H

<u> </u> <u> </u> <u> </u> <u> </u>   <u> </u> <u> </u> <u> </u> <u> </u>
 G   S   Z   G   D   R   O   O

<u> </u> <u> </u> <u> </u> <u> </u>.
 O   Z   H   G

4. <u> </u> <u> </u> <u> </u> <u> </u> <u> </u> <u> </u> <u> </u>
   I   V   X   B   X   O   V

<u> </u> <u> </u> <u> </u> <u> </u> <u> </u> <u> </u>.
 G   S   R   M   T   H

Can you think of ways to end our garbage problem? Write one way in code below. Have your friends crack your code. Then they'll know your idea!

_____

_____

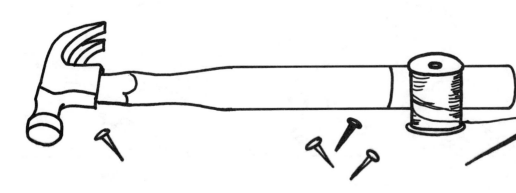

BACK TO THE SOIL

NEW WORD: BIODEGRADABLE

Some things can return to the soil easily. In a short time they "fall" apart. Then they become part of the land. They are not harmful to the environment. These things are called *biodegradable*. Other things do not become part of the soil. These things can cause pollution.

Look at the picture below.

Find the biodegradable things. Color them yellow.

Find the things that can cause pollution. Color them red.

GA1338

Did you find seven things that can cause pollution? Write them on the chart. Then look at the time line. Find each one on it. How long will it take to return to the soil? Write the number on the chart.

Things That Are *Not* Biodegradable   **The Time It Takes for It to Return to the Soil**

1. _____   _____
2. _____   _____
3. _____   _____
4. _____   _____
5. _____   _____
6. _____   _____
7. _____   _____

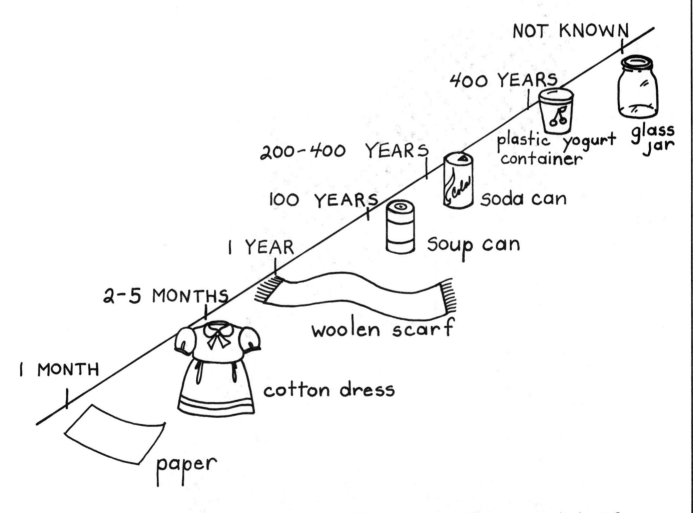

NOT KNOWN

400 YEARS

plastic yogurt container

glass jar

200-400 YEARS

100 YEARS

soda can

1 YEAR

Soup can

2-5 MONTHS

woolen scarf

1 MONTH

cotton dress

paper

Did you see the animals in the picture? Did you see the trees and plants? Can the things that are *not* biodegradable harm the animals? Can they harm the plants and trees? Think about it and discuss it with your friends.

USE IT AGAIN!

NEW WORD: RECYCLE

Look at the can on this page. It is empty now. Some people would throw it away. Other people would find a way to use it again. Using it again means to *recycle* it. There is more than one way to recycle. You can find another use for it.

Here is one way to recycle the can.

Can you think of another?

Look at the pictures below. Each one is something that somebody wanted to throw away. Read how you could recycle it. Then think of another way to recycle. Draw a picture to show how you would recycle each one.

	Use it to hold water.	
	Cut it into paper dolls.	
	Knit something else with yarn.	
	A piggy bank with an opening for coins on the cover.	
	Cut out the pictures in it. Then paste them on another paper to make a picture.	

A SPECIAL SIGN

Do you see this special sign?

It can mean that it can be recycled.
It can also mean that it is made from recycled materials.
Always look for it on the things you buy.

Can you find all the special signs below? Color each package that has it.

Did you find all ten? Now look for the special sign in your home. How many places did you find it? Write where you found it.

_____

_____ _____

_____

95   GA1338

A SAFE PLACE FOR GARBAGE

NEW WORD: RECYCLING CENTER

Here we are at the local *recycling center*. This is a place where people take some of their garbage. Each type of garbage is put in a special bin. Can you find the five different bins? What is in each one?

1. Color the bin for plastic red.
2. Color the bin for glass blue.
3. Color the bin for paper purple.
4. Color the bin for metal orange.
5. Color the bin for clothing yellow.

WHAT ELSE COULD YOU THROW IN EACH BIN? WRITE THE NAME OF TWO THINGS UNDER EACH BIN.

Each bin is taken away after it is filled. The garbage is then used to make new things. This helps the environment in many ways.

1. We save natural resources by using things again.
2. It helps prevent certain garbage from polluting.
3. It makes less garbage for landfills.

You help stop pollution if you use a recycling center!

96

GA1338

HIGH HEAPS

NEW WORD: COMPOST HEAP

What can you do with a banana peel? What can be done with dead leaves? Why not make a *compost heap*? Never heard of one? Soon you'll know how to make one.

A compost heap is a way to make garbage useful. It is done by making layers of certain garbage. A compost heap makes very rich soil.

WHAT SHOULD YOU PUT IN A COMPOST HEAP?

You can add anything that grew in the soil.

HOW DO YOU MAKE A COMPOST HEAP?

It is made by adding layers of garbage. Each layer needs to be sprinkled with water. Add your layers until your pile is *three* feet (.91 m) high. Then you can start to mix it. Mix it every *three* days. Keep it covered. Keep it moist. It will be ready in about four months.

Have any worms? Add them to your compost heap. They will help it.

WHERE SHOULD YOU PUT A COMPOST HEAP?

Put it in a corner of your yard. You can build a special bin for it also.

Look at the compost heap below. What is in each layer? Look carefully. Write the name of each on the lines. Use the words in the box below.

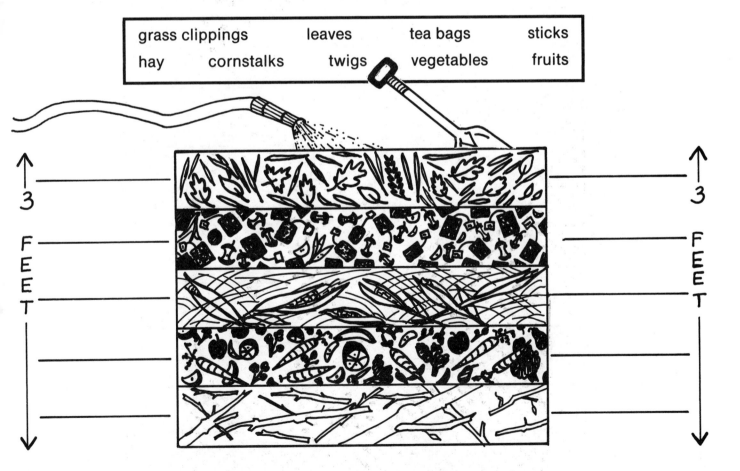

| grass clippings | leaves | tea bags | sticks |
| hay | cornstalks | twigs | vegetables | fruits |

Think about what else you could put in a compost heap.

GA1338

A SUPERMARKET SEARCH

NEW WORD: EXCESS PACKAGING

You're in the supermarket. You're helping your parents buy food. You have just picked this package of crackers.

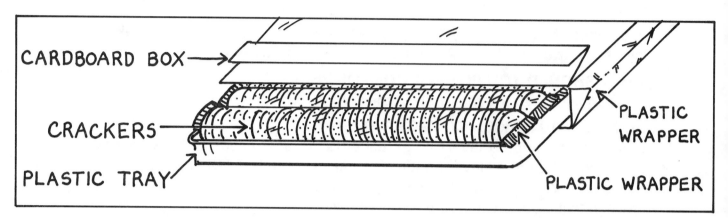

Do the crackers need to be in a plastic box? Do they need to be in a paper box, too? Do they need to be wrapped in plastic also? This product has excess packaging. Excess packaging means there are too many layers of wrappers. There is more wrapping than necessary.

Think about the garbage excess packaging will make. Your family may throw away about fifty pounds (22.5 kg) of plastic packaging a year. Can the plastic packaging be recycled?

Look at the pictures below. Can you find any excess packaging? Color the excess packaging red. Discuss with your friends why it is not needed.

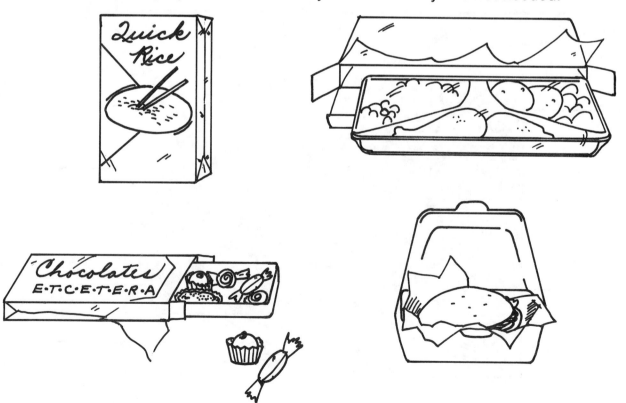

98

GA1338

You are finished shopping. You are on your way home. What did you buy? How were the products wrapped? Did they need to be wrapped that way? List five things that you bought. Write how each was wrapped. Was there any excess packaging? Write your opinion. How would you have wrapped it? Write your idea.

  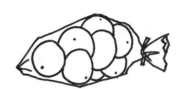

	Product You Bought	How Was It Wrapped?	Was There Excess Packaging?	How Would You Change It?
1.				
2.				
3.				
4.				
5.				

Read your list of products. Put a star next to the things that will become garbage. Can they be recycled? Count the number of things that can be recycled. Write the number below.

I could recycle _____ things on this list.

REMEMBER: Look for the packages with this sign whenever you shop.

GA1338

HERE IT COMES AGAIN!

Did you ever wonder what happens to garbage? First you throw it in the correct recycling bin. When the bin is filled, trucks take each kind of garbage away separately. Recycled garbage is used to make new things.

Plastic is crushed into little pieces. Then it can be melted and poured into a mold. It could be a mold for a new laundry container.

Paper is mixed with a liquid. It is reformed into new paper products.

Glass is crushed. It is used to form a variety of things, some of them quite surprising.

More and more products will be made from recycled materials. In the future, more materials will be recycled, too. Sometimes a product will tell you if it is made from recycled materials. Look for these products. Try to buy them.

Look at the garbage below. What could each one become? Follow the right path to find each after it has been recycled?

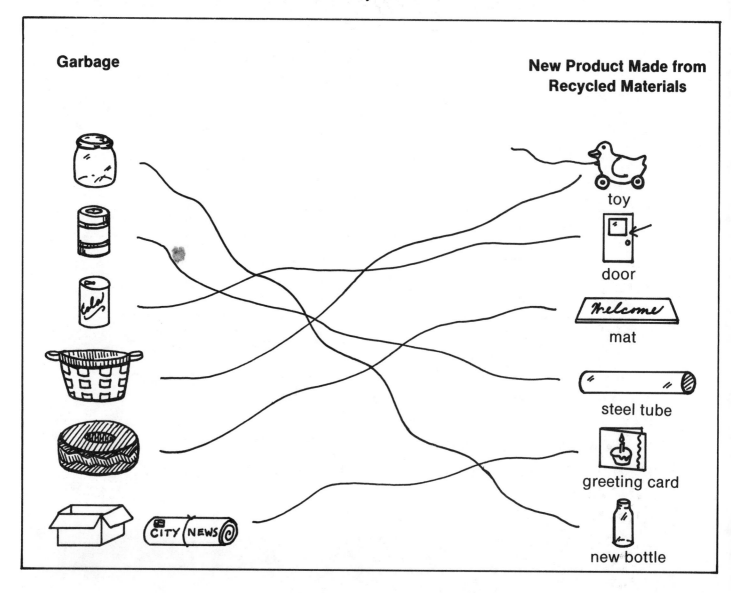

100

Garbage

New Product Made from Recycled Materials

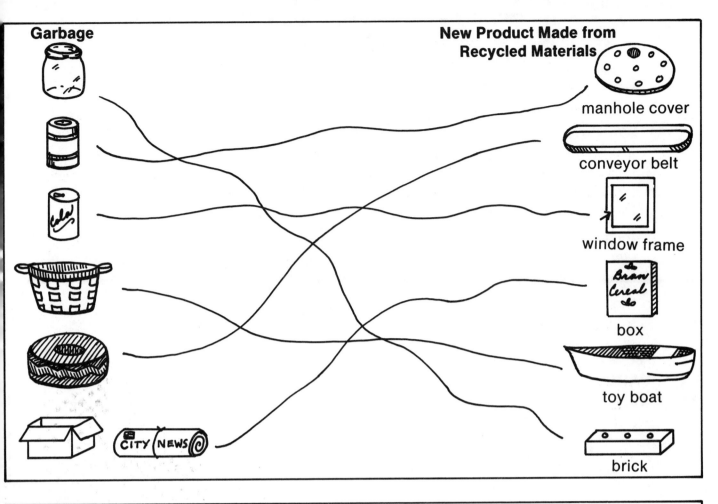

manhole cover

conveyor belt

window frame

box

toy boat

brick

Garbage

How would you recycle each kind of garbage? Write your answers on the lines.

New Product Made from Recycled Materials

_____

_____

_____

_____

_____

_____

GA1338

BURN IT!

NEW WORD: INCINERATION

You have recycled most of your garbage. The landfills are full. What can you do? You still have another way to get rid of garbage. It is called *incineration*. This means to burn it. The garbage is burned between 1300^0 F (705^0 C) to 2400^0 F (1316^0 C). Only ashes are left after incineration. Some people worry about incineration causing air pollution. Scientists are working to stop that from happening.

Incineration makes energy. Sometimes this energy can be used. It can make electricity. It can make steam for heating. It can be used instead of burning fossil fuels.

Incineration is done in a special place. Can you take this garbage there? Find the correct path.

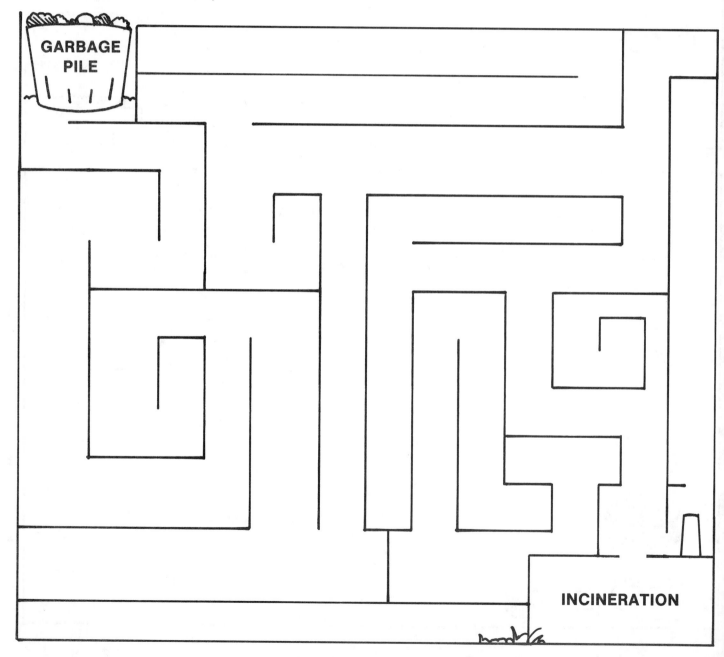

102

GA1338

WATCH OUT!

Pretend that you are walking in the woods. You see an open field. You run towards it. Suddenly you spot a large metal barrel. Something is leaking from it. What would you do? WALK AWAY FROM THE FIELD! There might be hazardous waste in the barrel. It might have spread into the field.

Tell an adult about the field. Ask him/her to tell the EPA or the police about the field.

SIGNS OF HAZARDOUS WASTE
- A container that has something leaking from it
- The plants in the area are dead.
- Nearby plants are drying out.
- The soil is an odd color.
- The water is an odd color.
- Dead animals are in the field.
- You smell something strange.

Look at the picture below. Circle all the signs of hazardous waste.

Do you remember what to do if you saw this field? Write it below.

_____

_____

_____

_____

You have learned about hazardous wastes on pages 54-57. You may want to look at these pages again now.

GA1338

REACHING THE RAIN FOREST

NEW WORD: TROPICAL RAIN FOREST

Have you heard the words *tropical rain forest*? What do they mean? A tropical rain forest is an area where there is a great deal of rain. The temperature is very high there also. This causes many plants to grow. It is home to at least half of all the different kinds of plants and animals in the world. Some plants and animals live only in tropical rain forests. It is home for some people too.

Tropical rain forests can only be found in special places. They cover only seven percent of our earth. This is a very small part of our planet. Where are the tropical rain forests of the world? They are not in the United States. You would have to travel far away to reach them.

Look at the map below. It shows where you will find tropical rain forests.

Find the tropical rain forest in Latin America. Color it green.
Find the tropical rain forest in Africa. Color it blue.
Find the tropical rain forest in Asia. Color it yellow.
Find the tropical rain forest in Australia. Color it purple.

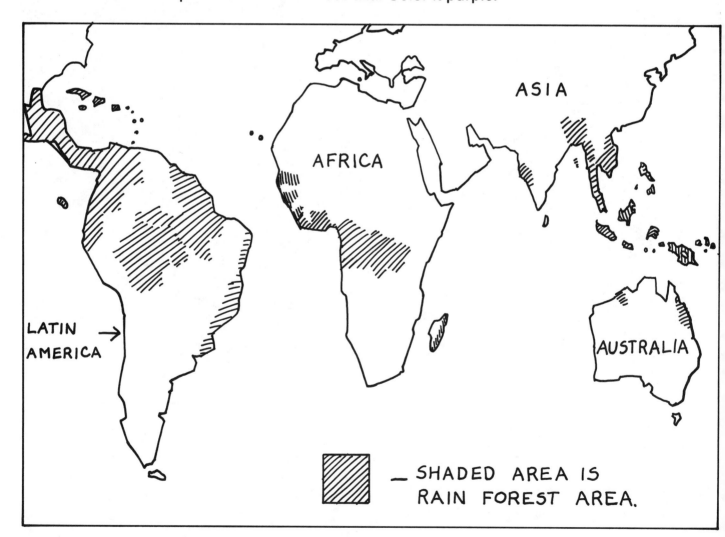

SHADED AREA IS RAIN FOREST AREA.

104

GA1338

SEARCH IN THE RAIN FOREST

Which plants grow in the tropical rain forests? Some of them are listed in the box. Search for them in the puzzle.

chili	banana	coconut	lemon	lime
mango	chocolate	bamboo	balsa	vanilla

```
C O C O N U T A
H B A M B O O C
I A B I A P R H
L N H J L S E O
I A K O S V W C
C N L L A T M O
V A N I L L A L
D E M M U K N A
F G N E Y V G T
L E M O N A O E
```

Which animals live in the tropical rain forests? Some of them are listed in the box. Search for them in this puzzle.

tiger	gorilla	crocodile	parrot	python
toucan	boa constrictor	hummingbird	jaguar	chimpanzee

```
S G J B S M E J I T N Y U B
B O A C O N S T R I C T O R
A R G G C R H O K G Z X W Q
F I U D L M D U M E B R A R
O L A L R A O C N R S T E N
P L R N W M P A R R O T L O
O A P U A O P N P Y T H O N
C R O C O D I L E Z S R L M
R S H U M M I N G B I R D S
T C H I M P A N Z E E P R A
```

105

THERE'S A PROBLEM

Right now there is a problem in the tropical rain forests. They are being cut down. Sometimes trees are burned to clear the land quickly.

More than one hundred acres (40 ha) can be cleared in just one minute!

You might think, "Who cares? I don't live near the tropical rain forests." Tropical rain forests are important to everyone.

Why do we need tropical rain forests? Add the missing vowels. Then you will know!

HINT: The words are hidden in the coconut tree.

1. Tropical rain forests help control gl ____ b ____ l w ____ rm ____ ng.

2. Some people have made their h ____ m ____ s in tropical rain forests.

3. Tropical rain forests prevent ____ r ____ s ____ ____ n of nearby soil.

4. Some ____ n ____ m ____ ls can only live in tropical rain forests.

5. Without tropical rain forests there might be fl ____ ____ d ____ ng there.

6. Some pl ____ nts can only grow in tropical rain forests.

7. Sources for new m ____ d ____ c ____ n ____ s can be found in tropical rain forests.

8. New f____ ____ ds can be found in tropical rain forests.

Now you know how important tropical rain forests are. Why are they being cut down? Unscramble the words. Then you'll know some of the reasons why. (Hint: The words are hidden in the python.)

1. People want to ARFM on the land.

   People want to _____ on the land.

2. People want to raise TTELAC on the land.

   People want to raise _____ on the land.

3. People want to use the trees for OGGLNIG.

   People want to use the trees for _____

106

GA1338

Many people want to save the tropical rain forests. Here are some of their ideas.

1. Plant new tropical rain forests.
2. Teach people to farm in tropical rain forests.
3. Don't buy products made from tropical rain forest plants or trees.
4. Tell others about the problems in the tropical rain forests.
5. Join groups that protect the tropical rain forests.

Discuss each of these ideas with your friends. Which one do you think is most important? Write why you think this.

_____

_____

_____

_____

_____

_____

You know why tropical rain forests are being cut down.
You know why we need tropical rain forests.
You know how some people hope to solve the problem.
How would *you* solve this problem? Write your thoughts below.

_____

_____

_____

_____

_____

_____

_____

_____

_____

GA1338

CLEAN THE LAND

NEW WORD: RESOURCE CONSERVATION AND RECOVERY ACT
NEW WORD: SUPERFUND

Our government cares about the land. We want to keep it clean. Many laws have been passed to do this.

The *Resource Conservation and Recovery Act* was passed in 1976. This law prevents the dumping of garbage in open areas. Now everyone must throw away garbage properly.

In 1980 *Superfund* was created to solve a major problem. Hazardous waste had been dumped in many places. The land was extremely polluted. Who would clean these places? Where would people get the money to do it? Superfund was the answer. The EPA finds the people who caused the problem. Then they ask them to pay a great deal of money. The money is used to clean up hazardous waste.

Many areas have their own recycling laws too. Sometimes on special days, only certain garbage is collected. Maybe on Monday the garbage collector takes newspapers. Wednesday may be the day that glass is picked up. In other areas there are recycling centers. Do you know your local recycling laws? If you don't, ask an adult to tell you.

Now you know some of the laws that protect the land. You also know some of the problems we face. What law would you write to protect our land? First write the problem you want to solve. Then write your law.

My law will solve _____

_____

_____

My law will be called _____

_____

_____

My law will ask people to _____

_____

_____

_____

_____

GA1338

RECYCLE YOUR LUNCH

Garbage is always left over after lunch. Is it the can that held your drink? Maybe it is the bag that held your sandwich. Is it the food itself?

How about starting your own school recycling program?

Here's how to do it.

1. Learn what things can be recycled in your neighborhood.
2. Plan your school recycling center.
3. Get the permission of your teacher and school principal.
4. Get your friends to help you.
5. Set up bins for plastic, bottles, paper and food. Label them.
6. Plan ways to teach others about recycling.
7. Have people put their garbage in the right bins. (Ask people to rinse bottles and cans. This stops odors.)
8. Set up a compost heap at your school for food. (Directions on page 97.)
9. Arrange for adults to take the different bins to a larger recycling center.

Draw your recycling center in the space below. Think about these questions before you begin.

- Where will you put each bin?
- How will the bins be emptied?
- What will you use for real bins?
- Who will run the recycling center?
- Who will explain how the center works?

Then present your ideas to your teacher and principal. Explain why you want to set up a recycling center. Describe how it will work. Good luck!

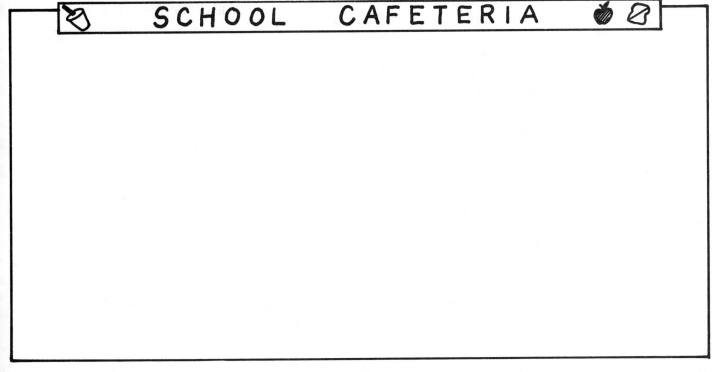

SCHOOL CAFETERIA

GA1338

PAPER RECYCLING

Do you always need a recycling center to recycle? No! You can recycle paper by yourself. You will have a new piece of paper. Here is how to do it!

WHAT YOU WILL NEED

old newspaper
water
one large roasting pan
one large wooden spoon

one piece of screen
two old towels
heavy bricks or rocks

WHAT YOU SHOULD DO

PREPARING

1. Tear up some newspapers.
2. Put them in the pail.
3. Cover them with water.
4. Mix the paper and water together.
5. Let this soak for twelve hours (or until paper is just about falling apart).

MIXING PAPER AND WATER

1. Pour out the extra water.
2. Use your spoon to stir the wet paper. Keep doing this until it looks soft. It should almost stick together. This is called "pulp."
3. Add an equal amount of water and pulp. Mix together.
4. Put the screen in the "pulp."

MAKING THE PAPER

1. Spread out the towel.
2. Lift the screen with "pulp" on it out of the pan.
3. Place it on the towel. *Make sure the "pulp" side is facing the towel.*
4. Press on the screen.
5. Lift off the screen.
6. Place the other towel on top of the "pulp."
7. Press on it.
8. Put the rocks or bricks on it.
9. Wait a few hours. Your "pulp" will turn to paper.
10. Peel the paper from the towel.
11. Let your paper dry completely on newspaper.

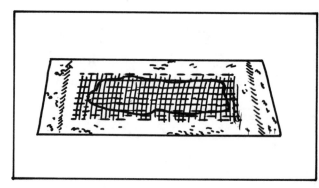

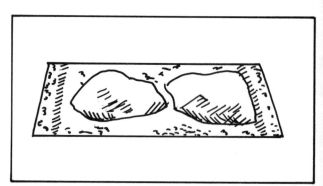

Here's an idea! Make greeting cards using your own recycled paper. Can you think of other uses for your recycled paper?

GA1336

CHECK IT OFF!

How can you protect our land? Here are some ideas. Are you already doing some of these? Check off each action as you do it. Try to do everything on the list. Add some new ideas to it.

Make a large poster using these ideas. Maybe you can hang it in the library. Can you put it in the window of a store? Show the list to everyone you know. We can protect our land. Each person can make a difference.

☐ Recycle everything that can be recycled.

☐ Don't litter.

☐ Add to a compost heap.

☐ Buy drinks in containers that can be recycled.

☐ Bring your own bag to carry home things from the store.

☐ Use both sides of a piece of paper.

☐ Buy things made from recycled materials.

☐ Don't buy products that have excess packaging.

☐ Find new uses for things that you might throw away.

☐ Share your ways of protecting our planet with others.

☐ Wrap gifts with used paper (newspaper, paper bags or used wrapping paper).

☐ Write to the people who make the laws. Let them know that you want to protect our planet.

☐ Buy things that will last.

☐ Don't use paper and plastic dishes.

☐ Wash a piece of aluminum foil or plastic wrap. Use it again.

☐ _____

_____

☐ _____

_____

☐ _____

_____

GA1338

LAND LOVERS

There are many groups working to protect the land. These people try to find answers to our problems. How can they end our garbage problem? Some of the groups are listed below.

Ecology Center
1403 Addison Street
Berkeley, CA 04702

This group helps people learn about our environmental problems. They also have recycling programs.

Keep America Beautiful
Mill River Plaza
9 West Broad Street
Stamford, CT 06902

This group works to "Keep America Beautiful." They try to get everyone to work together.

Waste Watch
P.O. Box 39185
Washington, D.C. 20016

This group gives information about waste. They help people learn about waste problems. They try to get people involved in finding the answers.

Choose one of these groups. Make a poster for them. Write the name of the group on it. Then draw a picture that shows our land. Maybe you want to show a problem. You may want to show our planet without pollution. When you are finished, send it to that group.

GA1338

PROTECTORS OF THE PLANET

Now you know many ways to protect the land. Complete the following awards. Then cut them out. Color them too. Give one to each person who deserves one.

Complete the list on page 114 by writing the name of the person and the reason for the award. If possible, hang up the list and encourage others to read it.

This award is presented for protecting our air.

Name _____

Action taken _____

_____

_____

This award is presented for protecting our air.

Name _____

Action taken _____

_____

_____

This award is presented for protecting our air.

Name _____

Action taken _____

_____

_____

This award is presented for protecting our air.

Name _____

Action taken _____

_____

_____

GA1338

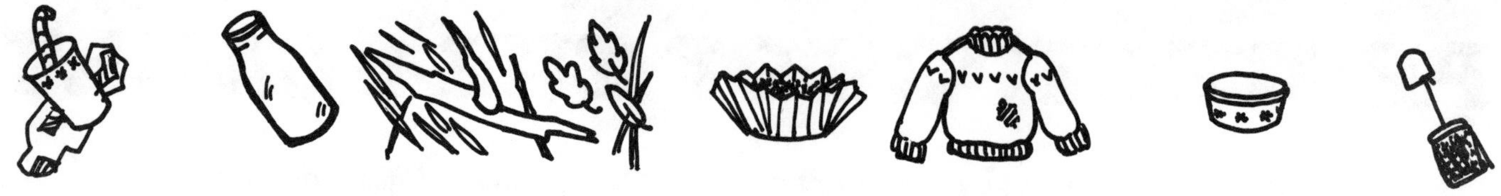

Name

Reason for Award

_____

_____

_____

_____

_____

_____

_____

_____

_____

_____

_____

_____

_____

_____

_____

_____

_____

_____

GA1338

IMAGINE

Imagine a world without polluted land. How would it be different from the world now? Write about a world without pollution.

You know how people can protect the land; you learned how our land is harmed. You know that

- garbage is thrown away carelessly
- erosion wears away soil
- excess packaging causes extra garbage to be made
- hazardous waste is dumped on our land
- tropical rain forests are destroyed
- our landfills are filling up

Think carefully before you begin. Remember that you want to protect our land from pollution. What will everyone do with their garbage? How will tropical rain forests be protected? How will we repair the soil? Would the world be very different? Imagine. . .

GA1338

WORDS ABOUT THE ENVIRONMENT

Acid Rain	It is a form of air pollution. It happens when certain gases mix with water in the air.
Aeration	A method of cleaning water. It mixes air with water.
Atmosphere	The air. It has different layers. Each layer has a different name.
Biodegradable	a word used to describe things that can break down and become part of the land naturally
Carbon Dioxide	It is a greenhouse gas. It is produced by the burning of fossil fuels. A small amount is naturally found in our atmosphere.
Chlorofluorocarbons	A man-made material that is causing a hole in the ozone layer to form. Also known as CFC's.
Chlorine	a chemical that is used for cleaning
Clean Air Bill	laws passed by the United States government designed to end air pollution
Clean Water Act	a law passed by the United States government to end water pollution
Compost Heap	place where certain types of garbage can be placed to make a rich soil
Environment	everything that surrounds you
Environmental Protection Agency	A government agency created to protect the environment. Also called the EPA.
Erosion	the slow wearing away of the earth's surface often by wind and water
Evaporation	the changing of a liquid into a gas
Excess Packaging	the unnecessary wrapping on packages
Fertilizer	a substance used to help plants grow
Filtration	A method of cleaning water. Water passes through things like sand or charcoal.
Fossil Fuels	Fuels found underground. They are usually formed from dead plants and animals.

GA1338

Fresh Water	water that does not contain salt
Global Warming	the rise in the temperature of the earth's atmosphere
Greenhouse Effect	A buildup of greenhouse gases in the earth's atmosphere. This traps the sun's energy. The result is an increase in the temperature of the atmosphere.
Greenhouse Gases	the gases that cause the greenhouse effect
Groundwater	the water that is under the earth's surface
Gutter	An opening on a street. It is designed to take away water that is running along the street.
Hazardous Waste	Garbage that is extremely dangerous. It can be poisonous. It can catch fire easily. It can explode. It can destroy things.
Hazardous Waste Disposal Center	A place to bring hazardous waste. Here hazardous wastes are thrown away properly.
Incineration	the burning of garbage at temperatures of 1300^0 F (705^0 C) to 2400^0 F (1316^0 C)
Landfill	a place where garbage is properly disposed of
Litter	garbage left carelessly on the land
Methane	It is a greenhouse gas. It is made by decaying plants. It is also made by animals.
Nonpoint Source Pollution	a form of water pollution that does not come from one specific place
Ozone Layer	A layer of our atmosphere. It blocks the sun's ultraviolet rays.
Pesticide	a substance used to kill pests such as bugs
Pollutant	something that causes pollution
Pollution	Something that harms the environment. It makes the environment impure or dirty. It can be caused by too much of a natural substance. It can be caused by man-made products.
Recycle	to make ready for use again
Recycling Center	a place where garbage is brought for recycling

GA1338

Resource Conservation and Recovery Act	a law passed in 1976 to prevent the dumping of garbage in open areas
Runoff	water that flows off the land into lakes, oceans or other bodies of water
Safe Drinking Water Act	a law passed in 1974 to protect drinking water from pollutants
Salt Water	water that has a large amount of salt in it
Smog	A form of air pollution. It happens when sunshine and certain gases combine.
Sewage	liquid and solid wastes carried off by water into sewers
Sludge	slushy material left after sewage is treated
Smog	A form of air pollution. It happens when sunshine and certain gases combine.
Storm Drain	a kind of sewer designed to carry away rainfall or runoff
Superfund	created in 1980 to solve the hazardous waste problem by getting the money needed to clean up the land
Ultraviolet Rays	harmful rays of the sun
Tropical Rain Forest	An area of the earth that has lots of rain and very high temperatures. This causes many plants to grow. Half the world's plants and animals live there.
Water Conservation	protecting and saving water
Water Cycle	The endless path that water takes—it falls to the earth, and then it rises back into the air again.
Water Treatment Plant	a place that removes pollutants from water

GA1338

ANSWER KEY

Is Air Pollution a Problem? Page 8
1. itchy eyes
2. hard to breathe
3. harm crops
4. diseases
5. harm outdoor objects that man built

From the Land into the Air Page 10

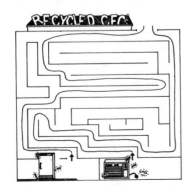

Crossing CFC's Page 14
Across
1. ultraviolet
3. chlorofluorocarbons
5. refrigerator

Down
2. air conditioner
4. ozone
6. spray
7. plastics

A Warmer Earth? Page 15
1. flooding
2. weather
3. water
4. live
5. farm

Hot, Hot, Hot! Page 16
The sun warms our planet. We feel the sun's energy as heat. Now our atmosphere is filling with certain gases. These gases change our atmosphere. They trap the sun's energy. They are called greenhouse gases. Sometimes too much energy is trapped in our atmosphere. Then the temperature begins to rise too high. The heat cannot escape. We call this the greenhouse effect.

It's a Gas! Page 18
1. Driving a car produces carbon dioxide.
2. Cows produce methane.
3. Refrigerators produce CFC's.

Trapping Chlorofluorocarbons Page 19

Crack the Greenhouse! Pages 22, 23
1. They use car pools.
2. They don't use air conditioners.
3. They ride their bikes to places.
4. They never leave the refrigerator open.
5. They plant trees.

Watch Out for the Acid! Page 24
1. There are no animals.
2. The trees do not have leaves.
3. The building is damaged.
4. There are no fish in the pond.
5. There are no frogs in the pond.

Traffic Everywhere Page 26

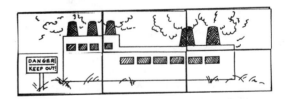

Indoor Air Inspectors Page 27
1. air conditioner
2. gas furnance
3. chemical fumes
4. cigarette smoke
Keep enough fresh air indoors.

Danger Zone Page 31

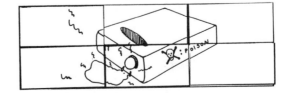

GA1338

You're Too Noisy Page 32
1. heavy traffic
2. loud music
3. old airplanes

Hiding in the Air Page 33

C	H	E	M	I	C	A	L	F	U	M	E	S
A	S	A	S	K	F	C	J	N	O	P	Q	M
R	T	F	B	R	C	P	M	R	S	T	U	O
B	U	E	L	T	S	D	Q	V	T	A	S	G
O	V	I	U	M	N	O	W	O	U	V	R	E
N	O	I	S	E	Z	Y	X	Z	A	A	B	R
D	W	G	V	F	W	X	Y	W	W	R	C	M
I	X	A	H	G	A	Z	D	X	N	A	D	N
O	M	H	B	H	C	I	D	R	A	I	N	A
X	N	B	C	I	M	C	M	O	S	S	D	S
I	A	C	D	J	N	N	A	V	Y	Q	A	W
D	C	D	E	K	B	A	E	W	P	R	B	U
E	D	E	K	M	X	E	M	Z	S	C	R	M

Free Air Page 34

Clean Air Actions Page 36
1. Walk to places instead of riding in a car.
2. Ride your bike to places.
3. Use buses or trains when you can.
4. Keep enough fresh air in your home.
5. Ask people not to speed on highways. Driving at slower speeds pollutes less.
6. Ask people not to burn fossil fuels.

Not the Usual Page 38
1. falling water
2. sun
3. wind
4. ocean energy
5. heat from inside the earth

Water Worries Page 48
1. fish
2. seaweed
3. people

Water, Water Everywhere Page 49

S	T	R	E	A	M	M
E	A	I	F	J	A	A
A	B	V	G	N	F	R
C	H	E	N	M	T	S
D	B	R	P	O	O	H
I	A	Q	W	R	C	K
X	Y	R	E	A	E	S
Z	R	M	P	N	L	T
A	M	P	O	N	D	U
S	W	A	M	P	L	R

Troubled Water Page 52
1. garbage
2. sewage
3. pesticide
4. chemical waste
5. sludge
6. oil
7. plastic
8. fertilizer

Under the Ground Page 53

Red Alert! Page 54
1. Oil leaking from a barge into the water.
2. Boat leaking hazardous waste into the water.
3. Person throwing poisonous waste into the water.
4. Waste flowing out of a factory into the water.

A Dangerous Search Page 56

A	C	L	E	A	N	E	R	S	D	E
B	A	U	V	B	C	D	E	F	M	P
L	G	A	S	O	L	I	N	E	A	A
E	S	M	W	M	N	G	H	O	P	I
A	M	O	T	O	R	O	I	L	Q	N
C	T	S	A	I	J	K	R	S	T	T
H	P	E	S	T	I	C	I	D	E	S
R	M	O	T	H	B	A	L	L	S	M

GA1338

It's Time for a Change Page 57
1. vinegar, borax
2. lemons
3. baking soda
4. baking soda
5. baking soda, vinegar

Runaway Page 58

Watch Out Below! Page 59
1. gutter
2. storm drain

Did You Know This? Pages 60, 61
James oiling mower
James painting a table
James pouring on fertilizer
James throwing garbage into water

What a Mess! Page 65
1. Machines gathered up the oil.
2. Stones along the shore were wiped by hand.
3. Chemicals were used to break up the oil.
4. People washed the oil off sea animals.
5. Borders were placed around an oil spill. This kept it from spreading.

Let's Go to the Beach Page 68

soda can, bottle, candy wrapper, oil barge spilling oil, plastic laundry basket, bandage, small boat dumping garbage

Drip, Drip, Drip Page 70
1. A sink faucet is dripping.
2. A person is running the water while brushing her teeth.
3. A washing machine is running without it being full.
4. A toilet is leaking.
5. A sink faucet is running without being used.
6. A hose is running without being used.

Clean and Clear Page 72
1. water treatment plants
2. filtration
3. aeration
4. chlorine

Helpful Ways Pages 74, 75
1. Don't waste water while washing.
2. Never throw garbage into water.
3. Don't pour hazardous waste into sinks.
4. Repair things that leak.
5. Don't put on fertilizer before it rains.

We've Landed Page 85
On top are leaves, grass, drops of dew on blades of grass. Next are droplets of water, little spaces that air might travel in, dead bugs and worms, bits of rock, clay and sand.

Use It or Harm It? Page 86
1. build
2. food
3. mine

1. plants, trees
2. soil
3. mined
4. hazardous
5. garbage

The Land Is Full Pages 90, 91
1. Use things again and again.
2. Repair things.
3. Buy things that will last.
4. Recycle things.

Use It Again! Page 94
1. Possible answer: a vase
2. Possible answer: a book cover
3. Possible answer: give to someone who needs a sweater
4. Possible answer: a container to hold small items like pins
5. Possible answer: give to someone else to read.

A Special Sign Page 95

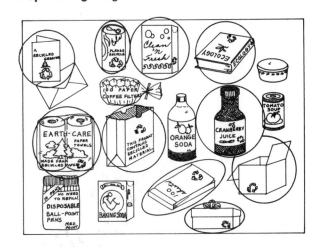

GA1338

High Heaps Page 97

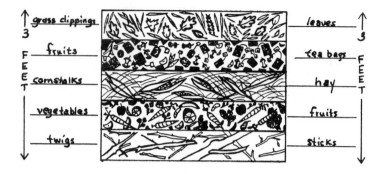

A Supermarket Search Page 98

Rice in a box with plastic wrap around paper box

Frozen dinner in plastic tray with a thin layer of plastic around it. In a paper box with plastic wrap around it.

Candy in a plastic tray, some candy is wrapped, all in a paper box wrapped in plastic.

A hamburger wrapped in paper in a Styrofoam box.

Burn It! Page 102

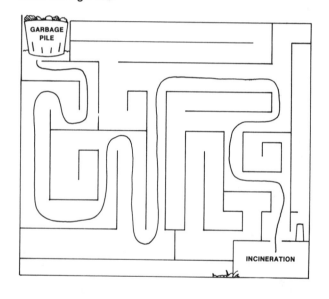

Search in the Rain Forest Page 105

There's a Problem Page 106

1. global warming
2. homes
3. erosion
4. animals
5. flooding
6. plants
7. medicines
8. foods

1. farm
2. cattle
3. logging

PROTECT OUR PLANET

A game about the environment for any number of players

OBJECT

To be the first player to reach the "Congratulations! You Protected Our Planet" square

GAME EQUIPMENT

1 gameboard, 108 Environment Trivia Cards, 24 Earth Cards and 28 Number Cards can be found in the book. You need to add coins or colored markers. Use these as playing pieces.

PREPARATION

Pull out the gameboard from the center of the book. Cut out the Environment Trivia Cards, Earth Cards and Number Cards.
It is suggested that you:

- Cut out cardboard or heavy paper the same size as the gameboard. Paste it to the cardboard piece.
- Cover all cards with clear Con-Tact paper.

Put the Environment Trivia Cards in a pile with questions facing up. Put the Earth Cards in a pile facing down. Do the same for the Number Cards. Gather coins or markers. Make sure there are enough pieces for each player. Each player then chooses a playing piece.

ENVIRONMENT TRIVIA CARDS

The Environment Trivia Cards are two-sided. One side has a question on it. The other side has the answer on it. Place the used cards on the bottom of the pile.

EARTH CARDS

Landing on an Earth Card space means you must pick an Earth Card. The player must then follow the instructions on that card. Place used cards on the bottom of the pile.

NUMBER CARDS

The Number Cards tell you the number of spaces to move. Place used Number Cards on the bottom of the pile.

TO PLAY

Choose who will go first. The first player then picks an Environment Trivia Card. He/She DOES NOT LOOK AT THE CARD. The player hands it to the person to the right. This person will ask the question. (The answer to each question is based on the information in the book.) Giving a correct answer allows the player to choose a Number Card. The number on the card tells how many spaces to move. If an answer is not correct, the player does not pick a Number Card. The game continues until one player reaches the space which says, "Congratulations! You Protected Our Planet."

LANDING ON AN OCCUPIED SPACE

Any number of players can be on one space at the same time.

TEAMS

You may form teams. Each team chooses a captain. The team discusses possible answers. All must agree on one answer. Then the captain states the answer.

123

GA1338

EARTH CARDS

You told a neighbor where to recycle motor oil. Advance to the nearest square.	You threw paint into your garbage pail. Miss a turn.	You picked up litter at the beach. Advance to the nearest square.
You saved water. Advance to the nearest star.	You dumped toxic waste. Go back four spaces.	You picked up litter at a park. Advance three spaces.
You cleaned up after walking your dog. Advance to the nearest triangle.	You helped form a car pool. Advance to the nearest star.	You put up an antipollution poster. Advance to the nearest triangle.
You wasted energy. Go back to start.	You read a book about toxic waste. Move ahead to the nearest diamond.	You helped plant trees. Save this card and use it to decline an Earth Card you do not want.

EARTH CARDS

You didn't use paper or plastic plates at your party. Move ahead to the nearest diamond.	You saved energy. Advance to the nearest star.	You didn't buy a product that has CFC's in it. Advance one space.
You reported a factory that was dumping waste into a local stream. Pick another Earth Card.	You threw your candy wrapper on the road. Miss a turn.	Hurrah! You recycled your soda can. Move ahead to the nearest triangle.
You helped clean the local stream. Advance two spaces.	You rode your bicycle instead of asking your mom to drive you to a meeting. Advance to the nearest square.	You helped to set up a recycling center. Save this card and use it to decline an Earth Card you do not want.
You bought a card made from recycled paper. Pick another Earth Card.	You didn't turn off the water while brushing your teeth. Miss a turn.	You started your own compost heap. Move ahead to the nearest star.

NUMBER CARDS

Move 1 space.	Move 2 spaces.	Move 3 spaces.	Move 4 spaces.
Move 1 space.	Move 2 spaces.	Move 3 spaces.	Move 4 spaces.
Move 1 space.	Move 2 spaces.	Move 3 spaces.	Move 4 spaces.
Move 1 space.	Move 2 spaces.	Move 3 spaces.	Move 4 spaces.
Move 1 space.	Move 2 spaces.	Move 3 spaces.	Move 4 spaces.
Move 1 space.	Move 2 spaces.	Move 3 spaces.	Move 4 spaces.
Move 1 space.	Move 2 spaces.	Move 3 spaces.	Move 4 spaces.

GA1338

PROTECT OUR PLANET GAME CARDS

AIR ENVIRONMENT TRIVIA CARDS

What is the warming of the earth's atmosphere called?	Name a greenhouse gas that is made when a car is driven.
What animal creates lots of methane?	What is another way of saying chlorofluorocarbons?
What gas can air conditioners give off that is harmful to the ozone layer?	Name a fossil fuel.
What gas do fossil fuels give off when burned?	What do you experience inside a car that is parked in the sun?
What word tells how earth will feel if the greenhouse effect isn't stopped?	What gas do trees use to make their food?
What is formed when smoke and fog mix?	Name one indoor plant that can end indoor air pollution.
What is it called when gases from burning fossil fuels mix with snow or rain?	What does EPA stand for?
What can you add to a pond to save it from acid rain?	What gives off most of the pollutants that cause smog?
Name a way to travel that does not cause pollution.	Name two ways to make energy without burning fossil fuels.

PROTECT OUR PLANET
ANSWER CARDS

AIR ENVIRONMENT TRIVIA CARDS

Carbon dioxide	Global warming or the greenhouse effect
CFC's	Cow
Coal, oil or gas	CFC's or chlorofluorocarbons
The greenhouse effect	Carbon dioxide
Carbon dioxide	Hot
Pothos or English ivy	Smog
Environmental Protection Agency	Acid rain
Cars	Limestone
Using the sun, wind, falling water, ocean energy or heat from inside the earth.	Walking, running or biking (any means of transportation that does not burn fossil fuels)

GA1338

PROTECT OUR PLANET GAME CARDS

AIR ENVIRONMENT TRIVIA CARDS

What is put into smoke-stacks to stop acid rain?	Name one cure for indoor air pollution.
When was the first Clean Air Act passed?	How does the ozone layer protect the earth?
What moves acid rain from one part of the world to another?	Where would you find the holes in the ozone layer?
What do you call the harm-ful rays of the sun?	Why did countries sign the Montreal Protocol?
Why are some people buy-ing cars without air con-ditioners?	Name one of the main green-house gases.
Name one way CFC's can get out of refrigerators.	What can you plant that will help cool the planet?
When is acid snow formed instead of acid rain?	What word do scientists use for air?
What type of air pollution only harms our hearing?	Why did our government pass the Clean Air Bill?
Where are fossil fuels usu-ally found?	Name one problem that air pollution can cause for people.

129

GA1338

PROTECT OUR PLANET
ANSWER CARDS

AIR ENVIRONMENT TRIVIA CARDS

Keep enough fresh air indoors	Scrubbers
It keeps out the ultraviolet rays.	1963
Over the North Pole and the South Pole	Wind
They wanted to lower the amount of CFC's made.	Ultraviolet rays
Carbon dioxide, methane or CFC's	They do not want to use air conditioners because they have CFC's in them.
Trees	From a leak, during repairs or when it is thrown away
Atmosphere	When it is cold or when it snows
To help end air pollution	Noise pollution
Itchy eyes, makes it hard to breathe, harms crops, causes disease or harms outdoor objects that man built	Underground

130

PROTECT OUR PLANET GAME CARDS

WATER ENVIRONMENT TRIVIA CARDS

Name the endless path that water takes from earth to the sky.	Where should you take all your hazardous waste?
What is water pollution that does not come from one place called?	What shouldn't you do with garbage when you are on a boat?
What can you use to clean an oven that is not harmful to the environment?	Why shouldn't you throw hazardous waste into your sink?
What is the water under the earth's surface called?	What words mean "saving and protecting water"?
What do you call a waste that can poison or burn you?	When shouldn't you fertilize your lawn?
Why shouldn't you run a dishwasher that is not filled?	How are oil spills caused?
How much water can be saved if you shower for less than five minutes?	What happens at a hazardous waste disposal center?
Where can dirty water be cleaned?	What is the name of the law passed in 1972 to protect our water?
What do you call the water that travels along the land?	What government agency makes sure people obey water protection laws?

PROTECT OUR PLANET
ANSWER CARDS

WATER ENVIRONMENT TRIVIA CARDS

Hazardous waste disposal center	The water cycle
You shouldn't throw it into the water.	Nonpoint source pollution
It will cause water pollution.	Baking soda and water
Water conservation	Groundwater
Before it rains	Hazardous waste
By accidents	It wastes water.
Hazardous waste is disposed of properly	About 15 gallons (56.7 l) of water
The Clean Water Act	At a water treatment plant
EPA or Environmental Protection Agency	Runoff

GA1338

PROTECT OUR PLANET GAME CARDS

WATER ENVIRONMENT TRIVIA CARDS

Why should you stay away from gutters and storm drains?	Name three places in nature that have water in them.
How can sea creatures be cleaned after an oil spill?	How much water is used every time a toilet is flushed?
What can you use to open a clogged drain that is not hazardous?	What is cleaning water by passing it through charcoal or sand called?
Why should you turn off the water when you brush your teeth?	Why can runoff be harmful to the environment?
What is the name of the first law passed to protect water?	Name two ways that water comes to the earth from the sky.
What do you call the water mixed with waste in our sewers?	What is used on crops to protect them from bugs? (It is a cause of pollution.)
What is the most common chemical used to clean water called?	Name a simple way to find out if a product is hazardous.
How does water rise back into the air during the water cycle?	What is the name of the law that protects our drinking water?
What is it called when air is used to clean water?	Name what is left after sewage is treated.

PROTECT OUR PLANET
ANSWER CARDS

WATER ENVIRONMENT TRIVIA CARDS

Ocean, lake, stream, swamp, bay, brook, pond, marsh, sea or river	They usually have polluted water in them.
About 5 gallons (18.9 l)	People can wash or wipe off the oil.
Filtration	¼ cup (60 ml) of baking soda and ½ cup (120 ml) of vinegar
It can pick up waste that it takes into lakes, streams or groundwater.	To save water
Rain, snow, sleet or hail	The Refuse Act of 1899
Pesticides	Sewage
Read the label.	Chlorine
The Safe Drinking Water Act	By evaporation
Sludge	Aeration

PROTECT OUR PLANET GAME CARDS

LAND TRIVIA CARDS

What is erosion?	What is litter?
Where did people put garbage before landfills?	What kind of pollution can garbage cause?
What does *biodegradable* mean?	What does this symbol mean?
What is excess packaging?	What do you call the place where you take glass, paper or plastic to be recycled?
Why aren't there enough landfills?	What is a compost heap?
Which one takes longer to break down and return to the land? • a piece of paper • a wool scarf	How high is the temperature during the incineration of garbage?
How high should you make a compost heap?	What should you do if you see hazardous waste?
What is a landfill?	Which one is more biodegradable? • a leaf • a piece of cotton
How much of the earth has tropical rain forests growing on it?	Name two of the things that are always found in soil.

135

GA1338

PROTECT OUR PLANET
ANSWER CARDS

LAND TRIVIA CARDS

Garbage carelessly left on the land.	The gradual wearing away of land by wind and rain
Land, air and water pollution	In town dumps or people littered roadsides
It means that it can be recycled. It means that it is made from recycled material also.	Things that can "fall apart" easily and become part of the land again
A recycling center	The unnecessary wrapping on packages
A place where certain types of garbage can be placed to make a rich soil.	There are not enough places to build new ones. Many old ones are filled.
1300⁰ F (705⁰ C) to 2400⁰ F (1316⁰ C)	A piece of paper
Walk away from it immediately. Ask an adult to tell the police or the EPA about it.	Three feet (.91 m) high
A leaf	A place where garbage can be safely buried
Minerals, water, air or things that were once living	Seven percent

GA1338

PROTECT OUR PLANET GAME CARDS

LAND TRIVIA CARDS

Name one of the places where there has been a tropical rain forest.	How often should you mix a compost heap?
Which one takes longer to break down and return to the land? • soda can • a glass jar	How long does it take until a compost heap is ready for use?
Name one reason why people should not litter.	How does the government get money for the Superfund?
How many acres (hectares) of a tropical rain forest can be cleared in a minute?	What word describes the temperature in a tropical rain forest?
How can you recycle a plastic container?	What does *incineration* mean?
What was created in 1980 to solve the problem of hazardous waste?	What do you call the paper and water mixture when you recycle paper?
Which one of these can you put in a compost heap? • meat • a banana peel	Which animal lives in a tropical rain forest? • a polar bear • a tiger
What word describes the amount of rainfall in a tropical rain forest?	Describe how plastic is recycled.
What is the name of the law that prevents dumping of garbage in open areas?	Which one should you put in a compost heap? • twigs • rocks

GA1338

PROTECT OUR PLANET
ANSWER CARDS

LAND TRIVIA CARDS

Every three days		Latin America, Africa, Asia or Australia	
Four months		A glass jar	
They fine whoever dumps hazardous waste in the wrong way.		It pollutes the environment. It can harm animals. It is ugly.	
Hot		More than 100 acres (40 ha)	
Burning of garbage		Take it to a recycling center or find another use for it after it is empty.	
Pulp		Superfund	
A tiger		A banana peel	
Plastic is crushed into little pieces. It is melted. Then it is poured into a mold to make something new.		A lot or a great deal	
Twigs		Resource Conservation and Recovery Act	

GA1338